Chasing the Green

Story by Craig Frankel
Written by Emilio Iasiello and Craig Frankel

Chasing the Green
Story by Craig Frankel
Written by Emilio Iasiello and Craig Frankel
Edited by Marie Hunt

http://chasingthegreen.com/

ISBN13: 978-0-9797075-3-7
Publisher: F.E.P. International

Most of the names of people and institutions have been changed to protect their anonymity. The events that take place, however, are very real.

For information write
F.E.P. International, Inc.
941 25th Avenue, #101
Coralville, IA 52241
http://www.fepint.org/

Printed in the United States of America

Preface

"Happiness is produced not so much by great pieces of good fortune that seldom happen, as by little advantages that occur every day."

- Benjamin Franklin

If you ever have walked the final gallery of the 18th hole at Pebble Beach, you understand the sanctity one feels when treading upon hallowed ground. The hole wraps around the Pacific Ocean as an idyllic testament to the game's intertwining relationship with nature, as if to separate the two would be impossible, if not irreverent. The ocean protects the left side of the par-5 fairway, the susurrus of waves crashing in a rhapsodic crescendo of sea foam and salt. Five hundred and forty-three yards from starting tee to the flag is marked with the most well-groomed lawn that has held more than its share of golfers in a state of genuflection, if not humility. This is not a realm for those weak in constitution or faith in their irons. If the Pebble Beach course is a cathedral, then the green on

18 is its lavish altar, an ornamented emerald set firmly between two sand traps, a constant reminder of what could happen. A sixty-five foot cypress tree guards par for wayward golfers, its jawed limbs spreading protectively over golf's most storied final hole.

The game of golf has been used as a metaphor for life, and in many ways this assessment is valid. At its most base level, golf is a game that tests not only a person's will, but also his capacity for addressing unforeseen obstacles that spring into his path. Hazards such as weather condition, trees, rough fairways, and sand and water traps all figure prominently into purposefully hindering a golfer's progression. Club selection must be evaluated meticulously, and each swing must be calculated carefully as to influence the ball's direction and distance. In this capacity, a golfer is not unlike any other profession. A golfer is a military general strategically planning his approach to each hole, tactically shifting to changing conditions. He is an artist whose many different swings resemble the varied brush strokes of a painter. He is a physicist implementing the scientific principles of torque and velocity to produce a greater amount of kinetic energy to drive a ball three hundred yards. He is truly Everyman and Superman combined, adopting the best practices from all other professions and folding them into his own unique identity.

However, this game far transcends physical or recreational activity. It is a way of life. The spirituality associated with golf is rooted in the natural world. When the golfer steps onto a course, he must shed all of his inhibitions and start fresh. There is nothing that he can take with him from his everyday life that will help him. He must recreate himself, discarding what he has accepted in life and start anew. People are reborn on the golf course; if your hands have ever worked the grip on a Ping G2 driver, you'll understand what I mean.

Although the game of golf, or at least some semblance of it, has been in existence since the mid-to-late fourteen hundreds, there is little indication or evidence that our Founding Fathers were enthusiasts for the world's greatest contest of skill. Granted, liberating the colonies from their sovereign oppressor and then trying to stand–up a viable, working, central government most likely impeded their ability to enjoy any significant amount of recreational time. Still, I can't help but think that playing thirty-six holes after signing the Declaration of Independence in 1776 might have cleared the heads of a foursome of John Adams, Benjamin Franklin, Thomas Jefferson, and Robert Livingston prior to them pushing themselves into completing the faulty, and ill-fated, Articles of Confederation. From my own personal experience, the one true value of a high-bunkered sand trap is that it has a way of reducing all problems into their natural state, and the fledgling nation could have bypassed four years of an inadequate and ineffective central government.

But golf wasn't in the plans of the greatest minds of that era. At the age of twenty, Benjamin Franklin took an ocean voyage back to his home in Philadelphia from London during which he used his time to reflect upon the future course of his life. The eighty-day sojourn would provide ample opportunity for him to compose "The Journal of 1726," the fruits of which constituted a thirteen point "virtue plan" that would shape and dictate his conduct and principles for the rest of his life. As history tells it, he would give each virtue strict attention for a week's duration before moving to the next virtue. After thirteen weeks, he would commence from the beginning again and repeat the process faithfully.

Of the thirteen virtues he transcribed, one stood out more prominently from the rest: Resolution. Franklin characterized this trait as simply the ability to "resolve to perform what you ought; perform without fail what you resolve." Indeed, it is this virtue that seems to have best distinguished Franklin's life for whatever professional challenges he embarked upon – author, civic activist, diplomat, inventor, politician, or publisher – Franklin demonstrated unfettered resolution in succeeding at them. He was perhaps the first, best, pure example of an American rags-to-riches story. Born into a modest Bostonian family, he lacked the economic and education advantages that would have solidified his position in society by virtue of birthright. Yet despite such shortcomings, he became one of the most well-known and influential Founding Fathers.

Growing up in New Jersey where I started and finished my formal education, my knowledge of Benjamin Franklin was limited to the textbook pages of high school American History classes. Never once did I pick up a selection from the voluminous body of work that Franklin composed during his lifetime. It wasn't until recently did I stumble upon Franklin's "thirteen virtues" and was immediately impacted with the prescient maturity exhibited by a man who was my age when I first started out as a young, impressionable entrepreneur. Although I did not know it then, I have come to realize how similar our paths to personal and professional success were, both marked with the innate resolution to endeavor what could be achieved through the willingness to venture into the unknown and the perseverance to stay the course. *Resolution.* It's that fine line that traverses the chasm separating success and failure. If you have it, falling is never a consideration; if you don't, there is little you can do to prevent that inevitable plummet.

So what does the game of golf and Benjamin Franklin have in common? *Chasing the Green. Chasing the Green* is golf vernacular for attacking each and every hole with an aggressive commitment. To have the confidence to go after what you want and not wilting before any obstacle no matter how daunting or insurmountable it may appear. In short, to give yourself fully to the pursuit. I can't help but think Ben Franklin would have understood the merit of *Chasing the Green.* If anything, his life demonstrated that you can achieve anything in life if you have the drive to do so. A man of little formal education and humble financial beginnings rose to become one of the most influential men in American history, for no other reason than he *wanted* it.

Chasing the Green. It's what makes anything possible.

I should know, because this is my story.

Chapter One

It all began in 1989 in Dallas, Texas.

To put this in some context, in February 1989, the Soviet Union suffered a humiliating defeat in Afghanistan by the mujahdeen who received covert CIA financial and material support, an incident that would set in motion the inevitable collapse of what Ronald Reagan termed "the evil empire." In June that year, Chinese students protested their government in Tiananmen Square. Two months later, Peter Rose would be banned for life from baseball. November saw the Berlin Wall fall marking the impending fall of communism.

But none of these global milestones mattered to me and, with the exception of Pete Rose's lifetime disgrace, which held personal significance, made little impact on my life or the course of events that would follow. In 1989, I quit college with a year left to go, and like many who saw the world of academia as a cage gilded with faux gold bars, I soon found myself in a place that I didn't envision for myself. While college had its merits, they were not mine. Simply, I wanted to expedite my journey toward success, whatever that turned out to be. Like many of the other self-made people before me, I had dreams of where I saw myself and the luxurious accoutrements that accompanied such a social and professional position. Yet true to the cliché of seeing four years of higher learning as an unnecessary obstacle to success, lack of any completed formal education severely limited my aspirations to career enhancement. With few opportunities affording themselves to me, I bided my time as a manager at the local Andy's Subs that specialized in fast food. As you can imagine, managing an establishment whose patrons consisted of mostly acne marked kids was not the most challenging or financially rewarding occupation, especially for an ambitious person who aspired to enjoy the finer things in life. My days were spent placating unruly customers, adjusting work schedules, and cracking the whip on the teenage staff who had a penchant for gossiping at the drink machine and sneaking free food to half the high schools in the greater Dallas area. A Donald Trump existence this was not.

Still, it wasn't until the regional Vice President made an unexpected visit that a plan began to formulate. I watched the manager take him on a tour of the seating area, the restrooms, and the kitchen area, extremely cognizant of how his tailored suit stuck out amidst the throng of denim and polyester. If this was to be my lot in life, it was going to be a lot in a high-end wealthy district with two cars and a swimming pool. I had already worked my way up from assistant manager to first assistant surpassing others who had more experience but less inclination to show the extra effort. The next logical step was to assume the manager's slot, to be in the position to instill change on the operational level, to receive bonuses, and bathe in senior management appreciation. But seeing the VP show up that day, there was only one true move to make: become a corporate officer to be an integral voice in all decision making. Don't get me wrong. A company car, country club memberships, a six figure salary – these were all welcome perks. In this world, everything was handed to you on a silver plate, and it was all you could eat. But to wield influence and shape the direction of the business, well, that was true power. You just had to have the drive to achieve it. Being young and hungry, it didn't seem out of the realm of possibility.

So that was my plan. I started to work twelve-hour days. A manager needed me to cover a shift? I was there. Open and close in the same day? No problem. Someone needed to be terminated? Give me the axe, and I'll show him the door. I lived and breathed the operation. I ate most of my meals there. My photograph was featured prominently on the Employee of the Month wall more than anyone else's. The brutal hours and lack of any semblance of a social life, these were all a part of this critical transition period. Still, I couldn't help but wonder when my opportunity for success –

real success – would present itself. The question that lingered with me day and night was: when would my chance come along?

Chapter Two

The road to Dallas came by way of Clark, New Jersey.

If you have ever ridden on the 172 mile snaking asphalt ribbon of the Garden State Parkway, you most likely passed Clark, New Jersey, a sleepy township nestled in the heart of Union County. In 1945, suburbanization coupled with the post-World War II influx of returning soldiers increased the need for more automobiles. Car sales in New Jersey, as in most parts of the U.S., swelled in unprecedented proportions. A simple equation soon developed: people plus cars equaled congestion. And in keeping with the U.S.'s penchant for addressing and overcoming difficult challenges, new roads were carved out of the environment to meet the newfound demand, the freedom of the open road becoming an extended metaphoric symbol for the U.S. victory against the Germans and Japanese.

The Parkway's conception was rooted in facilitating connecting inhabitants of northern New Jersey with the resort areas on the Atlantic coast, while alleviating the growing congestion that plagued the major north-south routes of US 1, US 9, and NJ 35. Between 1946 and 1959, engineers carefully constructed the Parkway with the eyes of artists and the concern of environmentalists, melding a man-made structure with nature. The "shore section" of the Parkway exemplifies these men's efforts. Trees were planted, and the only signs permitted were those for exits. Simplicity was the only guiding aesthetic.

Exit 135 off the Garden State Parkway funnels you into Clark. The township was named after Abraham Clark, New Jersey's delegate to the Continental Congress and signer of the Declaration of Independence. In many ways, Clark the town still resembles Clark the politician: quiet, subdued, and small. If you didn't know it was there, you would probably bypass it without so much as a second thought, the 135 exit sign yet another marker whose arrow serves more as a reminder of gas and fast food than a promise of something more.

Clark was initially established from Lenape Indian hunting grounds. The Lenape were the original inhabitants of New Jersey and Delaware. A sedentary, matriarchal tribe, the Lenape Indians concentrated on agriculture to supplement their hunting-gathering existence. As colonial settlers soon displaced the Lenape, Clark maintained its agricultural focus. Colonial settlements were loosely dispersed throughout the area, pursuing their agrarian livelihoods. In 1858, these settlements finally became an official community under the auspices of the city of Rahway. Clark remained a part of Rahway until 1864 when the 357 residents declared their independence and established their own town. Farming was Clark's principal business, but perhaps in prescient foretelling of things to come, the large farms were gradually subdivided into smaller ones. And when World War II ended, the farmers understood that a change was about to unfold. Land owners sold their land to housing developers as suburbanization took root in the very land that once grew crops. A new era was dawning.

I had spent my formative years – from birth to age eighteen – in that small, sleepy township in southern Union County. Clark was and continues to be predominantly white, with the next most significant ethnic group made up of Latinos. While not a remarkably affluent area, Clark maintains its solid position among the better towns in New Jersey. As of 2003, Clark was in the 65th percentile of the state income ranking. The median salary was listed at over 60 thousand dollars a year. Seventy percent of Clark's 15,000-member population was married with almost half having at least one child. A stone's throw away from both Manhattan and the ocean, Clark was quiet and idyllic. It was the kind of place where married couples wanted to raise their kids, even if the kids pined to escape the throes of suburban boredom once they hit their teens. Clark boasts good schools and low crime rates, as if both are testaments to small town values and a homogenous citizenry.

I was the oldest child of three; Martin was two years younger followed by Ross who was five years my junior. When I was nine, my parents divorced. My old man moved to Florida shortly thereafter, where he still remains. We don't talk. While divorces can be traumatic events that splinter families, they can also serve to galvanize them as well. They become defining moments where things can fall apart or serve as foundations upon which the future is built. Characters are formed during divorces, and they generally indicate how children will turn out. For some, divorces lead to countless, expensive therapy sessions; for others, they tighten familial bonds. In our case, it was the latter. Without our father around, the children became integral parts of the family, relied upon by mother to participate in the day-to-day operations of the household. Not only did we assume some of the functions our departed father once performed, but we also learned to fend for ourselves. Cooking, cleaning, organizing bills all became part of our daily routines. And we met these challenges openly. Responsibility was not thrust upon us; we rose up to grasp it ourselves.

My mother was, and still remains, the most dynamic and influential person in my life. She is an outgoing woman of petite stature whose heart is as big as the pancakes she made almost every

Sunday. She is a street-savvy New Yorker whose tough exterior is as much of her personality as her desire to bake chocolate chip cookies for us just because she "knew" we wanted them. Never once in my presence did she waver in the face of the divorce. Never once did she falter at the disappearance of the security that married life once promised her. Simply, my mother was and continues to be a fighter in all aspects of her life. Hard work was second nature to her. Countless nights over the dinner table she told my brothers and me, "If you don't earn it through hard work, it's probably not worth it." And as if to prove that she practiced what she preached, my mother attended graduate school in the evenings in addition to working as an administrative assistant for Texas Instruments. A single parent, she was *Chasing the Green*; she had the drive to succeed despite and in spite of the obstacles that lay before her. And like any great role model, it was her actions more so than her words that spoke volumes. When I look back at that time with the benefit of a distanced objectivism, without our parents' divorce, my brothers and I may not have grown into the ambitious, self-reliant men that we are today.

I imagine growing up in Clark, New Jersey was like growing up in any other suburb of America. The closeness of the community was evidenced in the myriad of recreational facilities scattered throughout town. Kids had their choice of several parks complete with baseball diamonds and swing sets to play at, and bicycles were their preferred mode of transportation. In the summers, if you were not from an affluent family, there was a large community pool to escape from July heat. There were even two golf courses that catered to the wealthy, older crowd.

Athletics were a staple in our lives. Being a household of three boys generally lured the other neighborhood kids into our backyard. Marathon games of baseball and football were held there, each of us pretending to be some professional athlete leading his team to victory in the championship. Games were intense but fun, the competitive spirit being cultivated in my brothers and me in our matches against our neighborhood rivals. Most of the families that lived there were Italian with names like Pecidini, Tropiano, and Dilolo. There were altercations, but fights rarely escalated beyond a downtrodden kid taking his football and going back home. These were the friends I'd carry throughout my life in Clark, both in and out of school, on scholastic playing fields as well as in pick-up games at the park.

My passion for sports carried over into high school. The best memories I have as a Crusader at Arthur L. Johnson Regional High School were as a varsity basketball and baseball player, the latter in which I earned All-State honors as a first baseman. That is not to say I was a poor student. I maintained a B average throughout my tenure. But I excelled on the playing fields that matched wills and talent in the spirit of interscholastic competition. Even now I can remember playing in an All-State baseball game at Princeton University in front of a crowd of thousands that wondered which of the players would surpass expectation and obtain the ultimate goal of playing in the Major Leagues. The shelf life of a high school student athlete is short, but while it lasts it is an incomparable moment where dreams are made and mythic glory is achieved. Even the school's principal had a soft spot for the athletes that graced his halls. Students revered us, teachers respected us, and come game day, more people could be found in the high school bleachers and gymnasiums than if the President of the United States himself came to town. Lasting friendships were formed by teammates who endured the two-a-day practices and the after practice shoot-a-rounds, a bond developing through repetition, sacrifice, and fear of not wanting to let your teammates down. High school sports teams are not unlike military companies where men depended on each other for survival, where in the heat of conflict a man is willing to go the extra mile for the person next to him. My best friend from those days was Joe Borden. He was an easy going guy who was tireless in his pursuit of athletic excellence and was always there for me in good times and bad. Even after I left New Jersey for Texas, Joe was just a phone call away, and he would always keep me informed on the gossip of Clark, the marriages, the divorces, who had children. Despite where our lives took us, we stayed in touch regularly, a practice that continues to this very day.

By the time I graduated high school in 1983, my mother completed her master's program and earned her degree. It was June, and she gathered my brothers and me in the kitchen where we had pow-wows affecting the family.

"How do you feel about moving to Texas?" she asked us, getting directly to the point.

My brothers and I sat in silence, her words hitting us with the full blast of a fire hose turned on to its maximum capacity. We looked at each other, no one wanting to answer the question. Martin was a sophomore at Arthur L. Johnson, and Ross was about to start high school that fall. The silence was indicative of how we felt. None of us liked the idea.

"What's in Texas?" I asked.

"A job. A better job. For me. For us."

Again the silence that settled was thick enough to cut with a chain saw. My mother didn't wait for a response this time.

"Change is healthy," she said. "Change makes the world go around. I've lived here as long as you have. Everything I know is here. But opportunity doesn't wait around for you to make a decision. It knocks, and you have two choices: open the door, or let it walk away."

"What about our friends?" Martin said.

"All you will be leaving is this old house and your friends," Mom conceded. "But here's the thing. There will be a new house and new friends in Dallas."

That night my brothers and I spent hours talking about it. None of us wanted to leave, but our mother had sacrificed a lot to keep this family sustained with everything it needed. She was there for us, providing for us, making sure we didn't want for anything, whether it was clothes, sports equipment, or a hug. We decided that night that this time, we would be there for her.

So later that summer, we packed up our things. As my mother pulled out of the driveway, our friends collected along the side of the road, saying their final goodbyes. Even Joe Borden was there, nodding in encouragement as only a best friend can do. I remember sitting back and staring forward through the windshield the way immigrants must have done when they sailed into New York Harbor, their eyes burning in anticipation of the new world ahead.

Chapter Three

The day my brother Ross came to me after I had finished my shift at Andy's Subs was the second most defining moment in my life. He was waiting for me in the parking lot when I left the shop. The first words out of his mouth were, "You stink."

Ross was nineteen. After he graduated high school, Ross dabbled in typical teenager jobs: he had been a bell hop in a five star hotel, was a stock boy at local grocery store chain, and even worked the front counter of the neighborhood donut shop. He finally took a job as a salesman for a cellular phone company, and it was there that he found his calling. Ross had the fluid gift of persuasion that could influence the way people thought, and more importantly, what they bought. There were more than a few cynics at the company when he walked in for his job interview. What could a high school kid possibly know about cell phones? Truth to tell, not much, but the moment he strode into the hiring manager's office, there was no question he would walk out with a job offer in hand. His job consisted of making cold-calls to prospective customers with cell phones and asking them if they wanted to switch plans for a better rate. Sometimes, he found someone who didn't own a cell phone, and he'd persuade him to buy one, as well as his company's service plan. Bottom line is, Ross could flat-out *sell*. It didn't matter if it were cell phones, hair products, or his capabilities. The trick was getting you to listen. And if you listened to him talk, you were drawn in. And if you were drawn in, you were going to buy.

Once Ross was hired, the company's customer base increased significantly, and it wasn't long before he'd risen to the top spot among the salespeople in the company. Career salesmen with over twenty years of experience couldn't keep up with Ross's drive and ambition. This is what separated Ross from the rest of the sales force: although his commission checks were substantial (the mark of a good salesman), he never rested on his laurels. He was always looking for a better plan or a different strategy. Success for Ross was not a goal, it was a God-given right reserved for those who were bold enough to have the vision to track it down and take it.

The day my brother met me in the parking lot of Andy's Subs, he wanted me to go into business selling cell phones and service.

"There's a huge market out there for this kind of stuff," he said. "We could make a killing. On our terms. For us."

I was not as much skeptical about Ross's plan as I was unsure of my own abilities to enter such an enterprise. I had all the faith in the world in my brother, but I never had worked in such a business before no less knew the inner workings of how such a business operated. Granted, day manager at Andy's Subs was less than what I envisioned for myself, but it did provide a steady paycheck. There, I had a plan, no matter how vague it was. If I were to join Ross in this venture, I'd be working for commission at the onset, something I had never done before. Doubt was unmistakable on my face. Ross read it immediately.

"I know we can make this work. I know the cell phone business, and you are a natural organizer. Together, the sky's the limit. Think about it."

Think about it I did. Over the next several days I did some serious soul searching. Each time I thought I had convinced myself to join Ross I'd have panic attacks coupled with horrible visions of being destitute and homeless before I had turned twenty-five. But despite the reservations, there was a more powerful feeling taking hold. The fact of the matter is, Ross's success had impressed me. When he spoke about the future business, his voice was firm with the unwavering confidence of one destined to achieve. And most of all, I wanted to be a part of that success, to get caught up in and ride out as high or as far as that wave would allow. He was that good of a salesman. I turned in my resignation to Andy's Subs the day my mind was made up.

Later that night my brother and I sat at the kitchen table discussing the initial stages of setting up the company. He was more professional than I had ever seen him before in my life. He had pages and pages of notes, things we needed to buy, two, four,six, and eight-month strategies. Listening to him talk, I almost forgot that this was my younger brother and not Donald Trump taking his first million into the real estate market. We were embarking on an adventure that would forever change the course of my life. Ross's dream became my dream. Tomorrow would bring a whole new world.

In 1989, cell phones were not as prevalent as they are today. At the time they were a business bordering on the cutting edge. In 1977, AT&T and Bell Labs built the first prototype cellular system. By 1982, the Federal Communications Commission approved the first cellular service for the U.S. A year later, Ameritech made available the first American commercial cell service. Five years later, there were a million cell phone users in the U.S. The mass marketing of wireless phone technology had begun. While the handsets were bulky, they soon became the status of the wealthy and visionary. I'll never forget the scene in the movie *Wall Street* where Michael Douglas used a cell phone on the beach to contact Charlie Sheen. Twenty years after the fact, cell phones resemble credit cards rather than construction bricks. In 1998, almost 104 million people in the U.S. owned a cell phone. With the U.S. population topping off at 270 million, there was a vast reservoir of potential clients who still had not embraced the technological revolution.

A&R Cellular, named after us, Adam and Ross, was our first business and was initially housed in a busy industrial complex in Dallas. At the time, the real estate market in Dallas was in the middle of a steady downward slide. Ross was able to secure us a prime location for minimal expenditure. It was a small office building that housed only ten business clients. Ours was a modest dwelling, roughly around five hundred square feet, with two front offices and a central space in the middle. At the onset, the office was Spartan; chairs, desks, and phones were the prominent fixtures. Here is where we began our entrepreneurial rise.

It was Ross's idea that we take on a third partner, and he brought in Bert. Bert was two years younger than me, stood six-feet tall, and weighed two bills. He was the consummate stereotypical Texan: a bulky man who loved beer and drove a pick-up truck. He and Ross had been salesmen together in their former company, and their friendship matured over hours of shooting pool and playing basketball after work. As I would learn later, business relationships were often started and finalized over games where prospective partners competed against each other in a contest of athleticism and willpower. In this case, instead of being on a fairway, I met Bert on the basketball court playing a game of "cut-throat." In cut-throat, three players competed against one another simultaneously. Simply, the one who had the basketball tried to score; those who didn't tried to stop him. It was a match where alliances where temporary at best, and everyone pursued their own interests relentlessly.

Bert was a guy's guy. Friendly and personable, he usually placed fun above everything else in his life. He was the type of guy that joked more than he worked, had no pre-set ambition, and couldn't care less if he had one dollar in his pocket or a hundred. Bert was the type of guy you'd call whenever things got too serious or you needed last minute help. While his jovial nature sometimes got the best of him, he'd be there if you needed him. He was a good addition to our fledgling company. But despite this carefree demeanor, sometimes Bert's good times went on a little too long, and his mischievous ways would come back and bite him on the ass. To illustrate, one afternoon Bert and a later addition to our sales team, Billy, failed to return from their lunch break on time. At first, Ross and I thought nothing of it. After all, this was a laid-back company where work and play were nearly synonymous. An early trip to the neighborhood watering hole was not against company policy.

A few hours later, we got a call from Billy.

"Guys? There's a problem," he said. "Bert and I are at the county jail. He got arrested."

"What the hell?" Ross exclaimed. "For what?"

"Shoplifting. Can you come down here and help us out?"

Ross explained what happened on the car ride over.

"Bert's a good guy," I told him. "But I've seen bowling balls with a sharper edge than he has. What do you want to do?"

"Mess with him." Ross's face creased wide with a smile.

"How?"

"Not sure yet. Follow my lead."

I said nothing and sat back in the seat watching the Dallas city glide by. I figured Bert was Ross's find and Ross's friend. It was his call on how to handle the situation. I was just going for the ride.

At the station we were met by a pretty female deputy in her mid-thirties with bleached blonde hair and a body that had just taken a turn for the worse and soon would be descending into full-time neglect. She brought up his file.

"Your friend was arrested for shoplifting a screwdriver."

Ross and I shared a look. We were stunned. He stole a screwdriver? What in the Hell was he doing at a hardware store, much less stealing from it, much less stealing a tool that at best would have cost five bucks?

"Can we see our other friend?" Ross asked.

The deputy led us to the waiting area where Billy was sitting, clearly agitated. He was stroking his palms against his pants legs over and over. When he saw us, his face transformed from utter relief to utter embarrassment. He immediately jumped to his feet.

"Thank God you're here," Billy said.

"What the hell is going on?" I asked.

Billy shifted slightly. His eyes lowered.

"It's my fault," he said. "I asked Bert if we could stop by Target on the way back to the office so I could get some supplies for my house. He was like, 'sure man, no problem.' So we stopped, went in the store, and were searching for the hardware section. I picked up some putty for my walls and asked Bert to get me a Phillips head. Some time passed, and he finally met me at the front of the store near the check out. I asked him if he got the screwdriver, because I didn't see it in his hands. 'Yeah, I got it.' I didn't know what he meant since I didn't see it anywhere. He just patted his pocket and gave me that dumbass grin of his. When I finally realized what he had done, the cashier had rung me up.

"Now the whole time this girl is ringing me up, I'm trying to be cool. Looking around to see if anyone noticed. And it looked like he had gotten away with it. I mean, I didn't see any rent-a-cops moving toward the exits or anything. But sure enough, the minute we step outside the store, security is all over our asses. We get escorted to the manager's office and have to wait there fifteen minutes before this old guy comes in and starts to give us the third degree, going on and on about how Target has zero tolerance for shoplifting and that they prosecute to the fullest extent of the law and crap like that."

I couldn't help but break a smile. This was classic Bert. He couldn't find his ass with two hands and a roadmap.

"So Bert denies the whole thing," Billy continued. "He's just sitting there shaking his head, telling the manager he was mistaken. Sure enough, the manager pops in a security tape and there's Bert on screen, shoving a screwdriver into his pants. They cuffed him and hauled his ass down here." Billy wiped sweat off his upper lip with the back of his hand. "He said you guys would take care of it."

We stood there a moment. I watched Ross, wondering what he was going to do.

"I still don't understand why he'd steal it," I said finally, trying to break the awkward silence.

"Because he's a dumbass," Ross interjected.

"Does he always do stuff like this?" Billy asked.

"That's just Bert. He's unpredictable. He never thinks of the repercussions. He just does things to have a funny story to tell."

"He's got a record now," I offered. "That's just hilarious."

The whole time the deputy was standing there listening to the story.

"Can I say something?" she asked. We turned to her. "When teenagers get caught for shoplifting, I tell their parents that a good way to stop such behavior in the future is if they spend a couple of nights in jail. Puts the fear of God into them."

Ross and I looked at each other then burst into laughter.

"Now that would be funny," Ross said. "Tell you what. Please notify our friend that we have declined to pay his fine. We'll see him at work on Monday, and if he needs a ride, that he should call a taxi."

"I can do that," the deputy replied. "Want to listen to me tell him the message?"

"Yes!"

We followed the deputy to the intercom control system. She pressed the button, and in a professional monotone, repeated our message to Bert. After a short pause, Bert's voice boomed back over the speaker, "FINE!" The deputy lifted her finger from the intercom button, and the three of us howled with laughter.

"I wish I could see his face right now," Ross said.

"He's probably tearing up. We should have told him not to drop the soap," I said.

In the end, we paid Bert's fine. He may have been a moron, but he was our friend. We waited for him outside as he was out-processed. As soon as the front door opened and his feet hit the pavement, Bert unloaded on Ross and me.

"Assholes! You were going to let me rot in jail over the weekend!"

"Cool it, Mr. Sticky Fingers," Ross said. "You can't do the time, don't do the crime."

We went back to the office. Bert eventually got over our practical joke at his expense. But as I look back on that incident now, I am chilled at Ross's words that day. "If you can't do the time, don't do the crime." I'd heard that cliché in a thousand B-movies and TV shows, but I never would have thought it would apply to me.

Chapter Four

Not every day featured such comical diversions. We actually did work hard and often spent long hours in our cramped little office hustling call after call, selling cell phones and service plans to the public. Because we were working strictly on commission, it was in our best interests to make as many sales as possible. Math was never my strong suit, but even I knew that no sales = no pay. It was an equation that I knew better than my own name.

Ross was the strongest salesman by far, and his commission checks were typically double those of Bert and me. Don't get me wrong, Bert and I weren't complaining. We were still pulling in a hefty income, and I was surpassing my weekly take-home check of my manager days at Andy's Subs. But Ross was the master. He had a gift to know how to read the voice on the other end of the phone. It didn't matter if it was a man or woman, he could react instantaneously to the slightest tonal inflection and adopt the best persona the prospective customer would respond to. He got so good that he could close multiple calls a day, selling to old and young alike, regardless of sex or employment status. He was a teenager making over ten thousand dollars a month by simply cold calling, the modern world's way of going door-to-door. A stranger is literally contacting you and asking you for your money. There is no harder business in the world. Ask any salesman. If you can sell a cold call, you have something. Ross had that something. And more.

This was how it was done. We started with a local area code and a cell phone number prefix like 972. Then we'd start dialing in numerical order: 972-0001, 972-0002, etc., and work the entire number strain. In several instances, those were not active numbers, as at the time cell phones hadn't flooded mainstream America. However, when we did get a person on the line, we went into pitch mode, informing them that our company could give them a lower rate than their current provider at no extra charge. If they were interested, we would call them back on a landline to answer any questions. This was important because if they gave us their home or office number, it was an indication that they were ready to buy, and as long as you didn't drool over yourself on the phone, the sale was almost a given. The art of the call was being able to entice the customers enough to want to call us back because we had something that they so desperately needed. Who didn't want to save money? Furthermore, what made the cold call even more legitimate – the beauty of the operation – was enticing the customers enough to want to give us their home or office landline numbers, which demonstrated our desire to save them money, as cell phone usage at the time generally cost on average thirty cents per minute. When we finally did call them back, the closing part of the pitch was that our company maintained more cell towers in the area for better coverage.

It was as easy as that. Deals were sealed and the company soon expanded. We typically tapped into our seemingly limitless reservoir of friends to supplement our workforce, people that were bright but didn't have anything going on in their lives. As profits allowed, we'd hire one or two at a time. Our office resembled a fraternity house with twenty-something men milling about or working the phones. Ross and I strove hard to instill the type of atmosphere we had always envisioned for our operation, one that successfully melded a "work hard, play hard" sensibility. We offered a tremendous flexibility in scheduling, which allowed us to expand the office's overall business hours and target a wider customer base. None of our friends quite ever achieved the same level of success as the original founding three had; nonetheless, they earned a comfortable living in an employee-favorite environment. While some proved to be competent salesmen, others just didn't have the knack or aptitude for sales and ended up leaving the company. There were never hard feelings in parting, and never once did any of them ever convey dissatisfaction with either my brother or I as bosses.

One of our favorite office pastimes was playing our own concoction of the TV game show "Jeopardy." Each afternoon, several of us, particularly Ross, Billy, and I, would gather around the small television on my desk and watch an episode of America's favorite and most syndicated quiz show. Alex Trebek's trademark smugness never ceases to make us laugh even to this day.

Our game went like this: each of us would earn a point for every correct answer we called out before the actual contestant answered. It made for a fierce competitive environment with people fighting to shout out answers usually resulting in arguments as a result of tie-breaking close calls. The first time we played "office Jeopardy" with the following score: I had five points, Billy seven, and Ross three. The category for the final question that night was "Geography." Knowing next-to-nothing about world geography, and seeing the show enough times to know that the final question was most likely catered to those who paid attention in school, I refrained from making a wager, betting zero points. Ross was more game, putting two of his three points into the pot. But Billy was too competitive, and a self-proclaimed genius, to bet conservatively even though he had the lead. He was an "all-in" type of person, and true to his nature, bet the farm.

We casually traded jibes at one another as we waited for Trebek to read the final answer. "It's the only state lying south of the Tropic of Cancer."

You could cut the silence with a dull knife. It was obvious that none of us had a clue, and we sat there dumbfounded as the jeopardy jingle ticked off the seconds for the real contestants. I gave Billy a cocky smile that said, "You just lost, chump." When Trebek read the answer, it was evident that none of A&R Cellular's finest had gotten it right, making me the first office champion. I thrust my hands up in victory.

"Strategy, boys. Strategy," I told them.

"You cheated," Billy protested.

"How did I cheat?" I countered.

"You didn't make a wager."

"Contestants bet zero all the time, Billy," I said. "You watch the show."

"It's not fair. What's the point of having a final round if you're not going to bet anything?" he said.

"Sounds like someone needs a juice box and a time out," Ross said.

Billy flipped him the bird and sulked off. Ross and I spent the better part of the afternoon trying to explain to the boy wonder that I had abided by the rules of the game. But Billy would have none of it. He took the game and winning very seriously, and while those were admirable traits in the business world, they can be a pain in the ass to deal with in normal every day issues.

I would soon discover that Billy's penchant for projecting over-the-top bravado was matched only by his compulsive lying. Nothing that came out of his mouth was the truth. Any time there was a conversation about sports, politics, movies, whatever, Billy would always find a way to top whatever story was told. He encapsulated the "anything you can do, I can do better" mentality. And you knew it was coming. He'd get this serious look on his face, eyes sunk back, chin set, and then start to spew the most outrageous, flat-out lies. While most of the time we'd just ignore him, Billy's constant yarn-spinning began to take its toll on Ross. He was like that mosquito buzzing in your ear when you were trying to sleep. You couldn't shake him, and you couldn't get rid of him.

One afternoon, one of our friends was bitching about having been ticketed for speeding the previous weekend. Naturally, this led to a general discussion about law enforcement and ticket dispersal. As always, Billy stepped in as the authority on the entire matter.

"You know," he said, walking over to us. "I got a friend who's a cop in the district where you got your ticket. It's not surprising you were busted there. They write a ton of tickets. My buddy says he writes about three hundred tickets a month."

"In that neighborhood?" our ticketed friend asked.

"Like clockwork. It's all about quotas."

"Wait a second. You're telling me your friend the cop writes three hundred tickets a month?" Ross interjected.

"Yeah."

"How does he have time to do anything else? What is he, a meter maid?"

Ross was never one to let someone pull the wool down over his eyes, and the need to expose Billy as the liar we all knew him to be spurred Ross forward.

"He's a cop. He does cop things."

"You're so full of crap, Billy, you're eyes are floating with it," Ross said.

"What's your problem, Ross?"

"You are! You and all of the B.S. that comes out of your mouth." Ross went over to the phone. "Tell you what. I'm going to call that station and ask how many tickets a cop in that town writes in a month. If you're right, I'll do your laundry for a month."

Billy just stood there. It was evident from his blank expression that his lie was going to be exposed. Yet despite knowing this fact, he couldn't bring himself to tell the truth. He just froze like a deer in the headlights, watching Ross dial the phone.

"Hi, this is Ross Franklin. I'm a college student at the University of Texas and I'm writing a sociology paper on the effectiveness of parking tickets in reducing parking infractions. I was wondering if I could talk to someone about this." Ross paused, as he waited to be connected to an officer involved in parking.

"Hello? Yes, this is Ross Franklin. How many parking tickets does an officer typically issue in a month?" He looked at me and winked. "Really? Now, would you say that was a slow month or an average one? What about three hundred tickets?" Again he listened to the response, nodding his head. "That's great. And may I ask your name? Thank you, sir. You've been most helpful."

Ross hung up the phone and turned to Billy and me.

"Not only would it be nearly impossible for a single officer to issue three hundred tickets in a given month, given personnel and material resource constraints, an entire station would be hard pressed to issue three hundred of them."

Billy's face flushed a deep scarlet.

"So what? Whoever you were on the phone with didn't know what he was talking about."

"You're right. I'm sure the chief of police has his head up his ass."

Ross and I burst out laughing.

"Go to hell," Billy barked out as he marched embarrassed back to his desk. Billy would never learn. Each time he spoke out of school, Ross was there to put him back into place.

This is not to say that every day was conducted with the protocols of an amusement park. Ross was always strategizing new ways to increase production. At this point in time we still made cold calls to potential customers and mainly concentrated on running the affairs of the business. Ross's forward thinking led the company to embark on two different trajectories that would enhance production: use of telemarketers and the acquisition of installation technicians.

The idea to use telemarketers came as a result of getting targeted by charities who constantly solicited donations to their worthy causes. While I'm sure most of the U.S. viewed such calls as bordering on harassment, the fact that these organizations continued to engage in such practices indicated that on some level they were successful.

When Ross first brought this up to me, I remained skeptical having been on the receiving end of so many telemarketing calls. Ever the salesman, Ross highlighted the distinct advantages of using telemarketers. First, we as owners could focus our time on doing what we did best, that is to say, finalizing contracts and closing deals. Second, telemarketer operations would undoubtedly increase the number of contacts and potential customers, which, given our proficient sales savvy, would translate into profits. Our business was a lucrative endeavor, Ross pointed out. We had to be willing to adapt with the times and adopt proven methods to continue to succeed in such a competitive field.

After a drawn out interview process, we ultimately hired two telemarketers, both attractive girls who were only a few years younger than us. In retrospect, we probably should have brought in experienced telemarketing professionals, people with the uncanny ability to sell ice to Eskimos. While the two girls were nice enough and definitely easy on the eyes, they lacked the killer instincts needed to boldly cold call and convince a complete stranger that he needed to purchase our product. Although this first foray wasn't as successful as we had hoped, it nevertheless provided us with a working model that we would refine as our business experience deepened and matured.

Ross's second strategic plan proved a more profitable venture. In the cutthroat cell phone business of the 1990s, it wasn't enough to just offer cheaper service plans to the public; American fast-food culture wanted their products delivered in a shorter amount of time as well. That's when Ross introduced the second phase of his plan, to stage a coup against a cell phone competitor and persuade one of their installation technicians to join the A&R Cellular team.

Now prior to usurping the technician from a rival company, A&R Cellular would have to schedule an appointment with the local carrier for whom we were working. This carrier had a fleet of mobile vans, but because were still considered a small company, we were not its top priority in servicing our clientele. Their sales-people would get first priority, and the vans would book up quick-ly. Subsequently, because our customers had to wait for the mobile van to program their cellular phones, A&R Cellular in turn would have to wait to be paid. Worse, it ultimately limited us on the number of sales we could complete every month. By acquiring our own installation service, we were able to complete the service in a shorter span of time and thus collect the revenue for services ren-dered more promptly.

Ross chose to lure Ryan from a cell phone company competitor because he was a guy close to our age and might be someone who preferred to work for a few young ambitious entrepreneurs with some money in their pockets and a reputation for treating their employees well. Again, Ross's keen business sense and salesman's experienced paid off. Ryan was offered a considerable raise and the opportunity to be treated like a person instead of a technician and have some fun in the meantime. Ross's plan worked so well that, in just a few short weeks, Ryan's schedule was getting so full that he offered to bring in a fellow technician, a friend of his, to help him out. In less than two months we had built and developed our own mobile van service and were well on our way to challenging some of the bigger cellular phone companies for area supremacy.

One of my responsibilities at A&R Cellular involved going through all the mail the company received and sorting through the myriad of invoices and payments from customers. One day, shortly after we got our mobile vans on the road, I discovered an envelope from American Express addressed to some person named Harry Huddleton. Since there was no one affiliated with the company with that name, I was about to throw it out when my curiosity got the better of me. Inside the envelope was a check made out to Mr. Huddleton in the amount of ten thousand dollars.

Ten thousand dollars, I thought. Now that was a lot of money. The check seemed legitimate and not one of those marketing ploys by the credit card companies. Questions swarmed in my head: Should I look in the phonebook to see if Harry Huddleton was listed? Should I contact the landlord and see if Harry Huddleton was the previous tenant, and if so, forward the check to him? On one hand, my conscience told me I should try to find the guy. But there was another side. And it was telling me not to look a gift horse in the mouth. My experience thus far had taught me that opportunity only knocked once, and if you hesitated to open the door, it was going to move on to some other person who might have the drive to accept what was offered. Bottom line was, if I could get the check cashed, I could pocket the money. After all, American Express would be expecting the check to be deposited. They wouldn't care who did it, as long as their checks and balances worked out. There was only one person who could plan an operation like this. I sped down the hall to Ross's office, waving the check like I had found the golden ticket for Willy Wonka's Chocolate Factory.

Ross inspected the check as I explained the situation to him.

"Looks legit to me," he said, his eyes widening with the greed of youth.

"So how do we cash it?" I asked him.

"We're going to need some sort of identification," Ross said after taking a few seconds to think it over. "The bank won't fork over this kind of dough without checking an ID or two."

"So we get a fake ID. We used to have them in college. How hard can it be?"

Ross smiled. He was on board.

For the next few days, we contemplated our next move. But the more we thought, the more doubt began to settle in. Fast cash was one thing, but this was a felony, a crime punishable by some serious jail time. Jokes about dropping the soap in the shower suddenly didn't seem as funny as they once had. When I expressed my concerns to Ross, he was in complete agreement. He suggested we discuss it with a third party, someone who didn't have a stake in this. Someone like Bert.

"Bert? If we bring him into this we may have to give him a cut," I protested.

"Maybe. But he's the only one here with the connections to pull off something like this."

Ross was right. Bert had associates who spent a lot of time in the shadows, whose business practices walked the line between legitimate and criminal.

"I'll look into it and get back with you," Bert said after we approached him in his office.

"Don't go forward with anything, Bert," Ross said. "We just want to know the possibilities."

"Possibilities make the world go round," Bert said with a smile.

About a week later, Bert brought the news to us. He had hung out with his friends and had scoped out a fake ID ring. They made quality product, he said. Top notch stuff. It felt like doing work with the mob.

"You know," Bert began. "My connections tell me we might consider selling the check for a good price. That way, it eliminates all connection to us, and they'd be the ones to face the heat if the false identity was discovered by the cops."

The new proposition was intriguing, particularly since it reduced our exposure. But reduction did not mean evasion. There was still a chance that the check could be linked to us if some determined police detective wanted to cover all the angles. Ross and I talked it over for hours. We learned that criminal activity was an exhaustive business. It made us wonder why in Hell would people want to pursue such an occupation.

The night before we were to give Bert our decision, Ross called me at home.

"It's not worth it," he said to me.

"I was thinking the same thing."

"We got a good thing going on right now. The business is solid. Money's coming in. We stand to lose a lot if this takes a wrong turn."

Ross was right. It was ridiculous to put our reputations and careers on the line for that money. We made more than that in a month. After I hung up the phone, I took one last look at the check then lit it with a match. I tossed the burning paper into the fireplace, watching it blacken and curl. Our foray into the crime world had come to an end. I wasn't going to be arrested for an amount of money that wouldn't even cover my bail bond. As I watched that check disappear into black ash, I was secure in knowing that I had avoided the only encounter with the law I would ever have in my life. Little did I know that I would be proven wrong.

Chapter Five

The first time I saw Lynn I thought I was going into cardiac arrest. There's love at first site, and then there's a coronary at first site. Lynn was very much the latter. She was that good looking, at least in my eyes. In the movie *The Godfather*, Michael Corleone's bodyguard tells him he's been hit by the "thunderbolt" when he first glimpses Apollonia, his Sicilian bride-to-be.

That thunderbolt was static shock compared to what was coursing through my body when I saw Lynn slinking around the pool table at Mick's, the local neighborhood bar.

Typically after work, Ross and I and some of the other guys would frequent Mick's. It was the kind of bar that most upper crust college kids wouldn't even consider stepping foot inside for fear of tarnishing their "on campus" reputations. But Mick's wasn't meant for them. The charm of Mick's was that it met the important criteria of the every day working class: cold beer and deep-fried happy hour appetizer specials. The genius of the neighborhood bar is that it has something for everyone: dart boards, television sets for the games, a juke box when things got slow, and for those who relish the art of pocket billiards, or as we say in the grungy confines of our local watering hole, "shooting stick."

Mick's had two pool tables with faded green felt in back, which provided spectator amusement for anyone sitting with his back to the bar. Since I occupied that chair most of the time (it was Ross's habit to claim the pole position and view the female talent as it entered Mick's), I was privy to some of the best and worst pool games in the history of Dallas. I'm not kidding. One time I had the inauspicious fortune to watch these two college kids play one game for *an hour*. I felt like I was in Dante's 10th Ring of Hell – Death by Poorly-Played Sport.

However, on one particular night, I was pleasantly surprised to see this woman with long black hair and smoldering dark eyes strutting around the table like a shark in waters where feeding is good. There were several things that caught my immediate and undivided interest: one, she was hands-down the most beautiful woman I had ever laid eyes on; two, she knew how to handle a stick – and I'm not being euphemistic here. She eyed up shots and played the banks like she was Jackie Gleason's goddaughter. Finally, and perhaps most importantly, she had a manner of carrying herself around the felt. I've seen women with tramp stamps (tattoos above the buttocks region – now a tremendous fad with women of all ages, 17 to 65) use the back pool room of Mick's as their own coming out party, flaunting their short skirts in the hopes of attracting every eye in the joint. Now this woman on the other hand had a certain style about her. Far from trashy, she embodied the gracefulness of the sport. Both hard and soft shots were released from her capable hands with equal aplomb. I was dumbstruck.

She was playing against a guy who looked like he sprung out of an Abercrombie and Fitch catalogue, straight down to his coiffed hair and glazed plastic smile. During his inane banter, she smiled politely until he missed his shot. Then she would pounce with the immediacy of a cat on a field mouse, moving quickly and confidently around the felt, her movements precise and efficient. She'd eye up a shot like an archer stringing up an arrow, hanging onto it just long enough for her eye to meet the target before she released. A soft crack of ball-on-ball and then – plop! The shot was made.

They played several games. He lost every time. Each time she'd beat Mr. A&F, and each time she'd laugh when he tried to regain his composure in a double-or-nothing bet. Even though I couldn't hear exactly what she was saying, I could tell she was pure sass – she had that way about her where she could ridicule you with a smile on her face that would make you come back for seconds on your knees, holding both hands out for more.

So you can imagine that when Ross and I entered one night after work, I nearly knocked him over to get to my usual seat as to preemptively avoid any philanthropic gesture he might have had to allow me to assume the "point" seat in order to watch the ladies making their evening entrances. He looked at me strangely, rubbing his shoulder as he sat down in front of me. When our drinks arrived, Ross was already somewhere deep into his post-work tirade: who wasn't pulling their weight around the office, the problems with his latest female "flavor of the month," and anything else that he had stored for later fraternal discussion.

"Adam? Yo, space cadet, you there?" He snapped his fingers in front of my face. "Anyone home?"

"What? Yeah, sorry. I was zoning." Truth to tell, my eyes were on the girl at the pool table, and he knew it. She had just set up a three ball combination. Judging from Mr. A&F's reaction, he did not foresee that conclusion.

Ross turned to see the action.

"Zoning? That's one way to call it," he said, checking out her ass as she leaned over the table.

"I heard everything you said."

"Every time we come here, your eyes are glued to that chick."

"I like the game," I protested.

"You like *her* game," he countered.

"So?"

"So go over there."

"She's with someone," I said. "Or don't you see that?"

"The person she comes with isn't necessarily the person she has to leave with," Ross said, leaning back in his chair. "Or haven't you heard? The thing with women? They're always looking to trade up. Talk, don't stalk, bro."

He smiled at me. He did have a point.

An hour later and a little bit of liquid courage in me, I walked over to the back room to get a closer perspective on the action. Lynn was starting a fresh game with a new guy that looked like he was Rush Party Chairman of a frat at one of the local institutes of higher learning. He carried himself with the demeanor of a person that usually got what he wanted, when he wanted. His body language was bold and confident, his smile directed at her in a way that was almost unnerving. He made no bones about his intentions: he flirted mercilessly, making comments to her that surpassed innuendo and fell into the boldly-rude category. Lynn didn't bat an eye at the overt suggestions, taking her time to gather the balls into the triangle rack. When he made a lame innuendo of the ball-racking process, Lynn smiled sweetly. Mr. Rush Party Chairman mistook her beaming white teeth for a promise of things to come rather than the covert warning of a wolf in sheep's clothing.

In all fairness, the guy was completely outclassed in both game and in trying to separate Lynn from her panties. He broke the first game but sank nothing. And then as soon as she blew the chalk of her cue stick, the game was over. She took him apart systematically, running the table in a flurried sequence of straight-on and bank shots, finally burying the eight ball off a harder shot than she had to make. Point made.

"Later, gator," she cooed, dismissing Mr. Rush Party Chairman after he had hovered a moment too long after his humiliating defeat. He sauntered off to his friends at the bar who wasted little time in riding him about the impotence of his game (much pun intended).

Lynn gathered the balls again and placed them in the rack. Then something unexpected happened. She looked at me, and I froze. I didn't mean to stand there like the village idiot, but what can you do? You stand there with your mouth open long enough, you're going to collect flies.

"Hi," I stammered out after a few seconds had passed.

"Do you play or just stare at me playing?" she asked coolly, arranging the stripes and solids in the correct order inside the wooden triangle.

"Excuse me?"

"Every time you come in here, you park yourself at that table and watch me play. You have your beer, and you look like you're oblivious to the words coming out of your friend's mouth."

"My brother."

"Your brother," she corrected herself. "So I have to ask you one thing."

"What's that?"

"Are you a doer or a viewer?"

The smirk that accompanied the dig was too much for me, and I laughed out loud.

"You want some competition?" I asked.

She leaned against the table and chalked her cue in a slow, deliberate twisting motion. It was a test. She wanted to see if my eyes were going to give her a long once-over. I held firm, keeping eye contact, and more importantly, trying not to show fear.

"Well that depends," she said finally, as I passed her initial test. "Are you competition?"

"I can handle a stick," I said, trying to sound more impressive than I actually was. I had good games and bad games. It all depended on which side my luck was leaning.

"I don't need to know what you do on Friday night."

"Were my blinds open again?"

She smiled again, and I felt my knees start to buckle.

"You rack, I crack," she ordered. "Yellow ball at point."

"What's your name?" I asked her, positioning the one-ball at the top of the triangle.

"You win, I'll tell you."

I lifted the rack from the balls.

"And if I lose?"

The question hung in the air for an instant before she replied.

"Business as usual."

The terms were set. With a smirk, she sent the colored balls all over the table with a resounding crack. The game was on.

Two hours later I hadn't won a single game. Not one. Zero. Zilch. Nada. The best I did was sinking four of my balls before she put me out of my misery, and to be honest, I think she was being kind. Yet, despite the losses, our conversation flourished. I couldn't help but think I was engaged in a modern-day Scherazade moment: perpetuating my existence on the table (and with her) by telling stories that made her laugh and kept her interest.

After she finished me off the last game (a two bank shot into the corner pocket – nice), I immediately started a new rack.

"Give it up already," she said. "You're zero-for-nine."

"I like even numbers."

"It's not going to help you achieve your goal."

"Well, you know what they say. A goal is not always meant to be reached; it simply serves as something to aim at."

She furrowed her brow.

"Who said that? A Salada tea bag?"

"Bruce Lee," I responded, shrugging my shoulders.

She broke the rack with authority, sinking the eight ball.

"Stick with kung fu, Bruce." She replaced the cue against the wall and gathered her things. "School's out. No charge for the lesson."

I started to scramble to stay afloat.

"Hey, can I see you again some time?" It wasn't smooth, but it was the only thing I could get out quick enough before she left. I didn't even know her name. Yes, I knew where she played pool most nights, but I wanted to take this outing to the next level at least.

"You got eyes, you can see me." She smirked and headed out of the room.

"Tell me your name at least. I mean, you kicked my ass. I should know whose foot it was."

She paused, looking back at me. There was that smirk again.

"Lynn."

"Another game some time, Lynn?"

"Are you a glutton for punishment or what?"

"I'm thinking of a different game. But it's still got balls you have to get into a hole."

Lynn laughed. The sound of her voice was like rain falling during a summer storm. Warm and wet and full of promise.

"Not pool I take it," she said.

"Better," I said.

"Yeah? What's better than pool?"

"Come with me and find out."

Lynn scrutinized me for a few seconds. Then she shook her head and wrote out her number on a cocktail napkin and handed it to me.

"You're on, buster."

About this time I began my life-long infatuation with golf. As a student of America's favorite past time, I never found golf to be an interesting sporting venue. Old men swung thin clubs to hit a tiny white ball into a hole hundreds of yards away. While it was a difficult undertaking, it didn't compare in my eyes to hitting a fast ball screaming at you at ninety miles per hour, or figuring out where a pitch was going to break over the plate. But the first time I swung a driver and crushed a ball two-hundred and fifty yards off the tee, I was hooked. It was a different kind of competition; where I was used to one-on-one feats of will, whether it was against a pitcher in the batter's box or a staunch defender on the basketball court, golf pitted me against my own weaknesses. Reading the breaks on a green or figuring out how I should adjust the wedge face to launch the ball out of a sand trap is addictive; there are no excuses to pin miss-hit shots. All of the glory and all of the blame rested squarely on your shoulders.

Sherrill Park Golf Course in Dallas became a regular venue for me and my brothers, and as in our days of growing up and competing against one another, we assumed the identities of famous golfers as we attacked the long, narrow fairways. Sherrill Park was and still remains a championship golf course originally designed by Leon Howard, a local golf legend who is responsible for planning the best and most challenging courses. Sherrill Park in particular consistently ranks among the top ten municipal golf courses in the state of Texas. When I wasn't in the office making sales and closing deals, I was out on the links trying to better my game. In this way, golf is similar to opera; you either love it or you hate it. It's possible to develop an appreciation for the sport, but if that initial passion isn't present, it will never become a part of who you are. To this day, I often return to Sherrill Park to understand the history of my love for the greatest game on the planet.

When the money started coming in, the founding partners of A&R Cellular found themselves in the obvious position of finally having the financial resources to purchase luxury items. Ross bought an expensive new sports car, I bought a new set of professional caliber golf clubs, and Bert at our pleading finally invested in a better wardrobe. But as you can imagine, when you're making money, there is an impulsive drive to make more of it, which explains why money is truly more addictive than any narcotics out on the market. It's the most fundamental of economic equations: you make money, you spend money. And the more you spend, the more you need to make. I doubt that principle is taught in college economics classes, but it's the reason why millionaires continue to thrive. When is the last time you heard of someone bowing out of the game after he's made a million dollars?

There are essentially two ways to make this happen: work longer hours, or gamble. I'd be lying if I told you that I wanted to spend more time at A&R Cellular. Who ever said on their death bed that they wished they had spent more time in the office?

For a time, I spent the better part of each weekend glued to the television watching college football on Saturday and the NFL all day on Sunday. As long as we had a remote, a phone, and a plethora of snacks, chips, and beer, I was in my glory. Bert, Ross, and I would call each other throughout these marathon game-watching sessions, complaining about calls or rubbing in the final scores of those games we had bet on competing teams. Sunday nights were reserved for a three-way conference to recap our bets and earnings. We each had our own special system to determine the winners, and while looking back now I can say in all sincerity that they were based on borderline ludicrous supposition, they seemed to make sense at the time. If I had to do a final tally, I can honestly say I about broke even. Thousand dollar wins were about as frequent as thousand dollar losses, and for a brief time, I couldn't help but imagine myself like the Robert DeNiro character in *Casino*, the expert at setting betting lines, savvy in all aspects of the art of picking winners. After all, his character was a smart Jewish kid with a head for making money, sort of the same way I thought of myself.

Eventually, the rush of gambling soon faded for me, as it was taking me away from the golf course. But Ross was a different matter. As my betting started to steadily decrease, Ross more than made up for my indifference. Our bookie, Johnny Llewellyn, became a fixture in his life, and soon occupied the "number one" space on Ross's speed dial. It was not uncommon for Ross to call Johnny on a Monday to get the lines and study how they changed over the course of the week to provide him an edge in betting come Saturday and Sunday. He'd read the papers from different cities to see how key players' injuries were, or if they had been arrested or were flunking school, anything that might swing the balance on game day. His betting practices soon followed the level of his obsession; he bet heavily, and he lost heavily. It wasn't long after that he found himself in the hole to Johnny to the tune of several thousand dollars.

"Shit, what am I going to do?" he asked me one day. We were sitting in the back of Bert's pick-up truck waiting for him to fill up with gas. "I owe Johnny a lot of money."

"You bet, you pay," I told him. I didn't see that there was any other option.

"I don't have that kind of cash on me," he said.

"So tell him you aren't going to pay." I was half-kidding, but as soon as I had said it, it made sense. It wasn't like Johnny was a hard-core bookie. He wasn't connected to any crime syndicate, although he certainly liked to pretend that he was. He was simply a redneck bookie who made his living on low-level bets; his whole operation consisted of people like us.

"Have you lost your mind?"

"No, hear me out. You don't pay him, what's he going to do? Take you to court?"

Ross rubbed his eyes. "He could break my neck for starters."

"He couldn't break his way out of a paper bag," I said. "Besides, he threatens you, you could have him arrested. He touches you, he's going to jail."

Ross got a look in his eye.

"You know, you have a point. What can he do? Besides, it's not like he hasn't made a ton of money off me."

Ross's trademark fearlessness was beginning to show.

"Look, bro, I was just thinking off the top of my head. I'm sure you can arrange a payment plan or something."

"Screw that. He doesn't even have any muscle working for him."

"I just don't think you should try to screw your bookie. Just because he doesn't have any muscle, doesn't mean he can't find some."

"Hell with it. I'm not paying. He doesn't like it, he can go kiss my ass."

Two days later, I was in Ross's office going over the monthly sales figures when the call came in.

"Where's my damn money?" It was Johnny. His pissed-off voice could be heard loud and clear through the receiver. Ross looked over at me and winked.

"I'm sorry, who are you looking for?" Ross inquired with a professional tone etched in his voice.

"You're late, and I want my money!"

"Are you sure you have the right number?"

"I know it's you, Ross! You have my money or not?"

"I'm afraid I don't know what you're talking about, sir," Ross said.

While Ross's confidence had always been one of his most admirable traits, it had a history of getting him into trouble. I didn't want it to get him into the kind that needed a hospital stay to recover from.

"You give me my money for those bets, Ross, or so help me God, you're going to walk funny for the rest of your life."

"Wait – this is about bets? I don't gamble."

"Listen, numbnuts. I know what you're trying to pull, and it ain't going to work. If I don't get my money by tomorrow, I'm coming after your ass. Got me?" With that, Johnny hung up the phone.

Ross put down the phone. "So, he's coming after my ass. Did you know Johnny was gay?"

"Give him the money, Ross. He's an ex-con for Chrissakes!"

"I didn't think about that," Ross said. His confidence was slowly dissipating. "Shit, what am I going to do?"

I told him for the next couple of days he should lay low. While Johnny wasn't like a bad-ass bookie you see in the movies, the fact remained that his business was based on collecting losses as well as paying out wins. If he failed in any of those two endeavors, his credibility would be shot. Without his credibility, he had no livelihood. Therefore, to preserve his credibility, an example would have to be made so as not to incur similar problems with other gamblers. Ross was scared. For three days, we essentially tele-commuted from the office, phoning in occasionally to make sure Johnny hadn't torched the place. On the fourth day, I ventured into the office. Ross stayed at my place since he was afraid that Johnny might be staking out his apartment.

A&R Cellular was business as usual. The phones were worked non-stop. Bert filled me in on the Johnny situation. He was nowhere to be seen. No phone calls, no surprise visits. I purposefully stayed at my desk during lunch in case the bookie stopped by. I was intent on trying to persuade Johnny not to break my brother's knees, even if I had to cover my brother's losses. But Johnny never showed. As the end of the day neared, I was convinced that Johnny was all talk.

But before I could enjoy this momentary sense of security, I heard a slight commotion in the front office. I got up from my desk and saw Johnny arguing with our secretary. When he saw me, he walked right over. Johnny was my height but burly, with a stomach forged from hours of drinking cheap domestic beer.

In my office, Johnny loomed over me as I sat behind my desk.

"What can I do for you?" I asked him.

"Cut the shit. Where's the other one?" he gruffly asked.

"The other what?"

"Don't screw around, kid. You're not that funny, and I don't have the patience."

"He's not here today."

"No shit, Sherlock. And he ain't at home. So I'm figuring you know where he is. You tell him when you see him, I want my money. If he doesn't pay up, he'll get dug up. Got me?"

As Johnny stood there, I took him in. He was an ugly bastard, there was no doubt about it. He had splotchy prison-made tattoos up and down both arms. But there was something in his face that told me this guy was all bark and no bite. He wasn't so much a tough guy as he was trying hard to appear to be a tough guy. The more I studied him, the more I realized that he was all image.

After he finished his clichéd laundry list of all the painful things he had in store for Ross if he didn't get what was owed to him on his way out, I quickly called Ross at my apartment.

"I just had come-to-Jesus meeting with your pal Johnny," I said.

"He isn't coming here, is he?" Ross said. There was tinge of fear in his voice.

"He said he was going to rip off your head and crap down your neck and blah, blah, blah. He's sure watched his share of mob movies," I said. "I think he quoted all of them."

"So what should I do?" Ross asked finally after a few seconds.

"Come to work. Forget about him."

"But you said…"

"He's hot air, Ross. He plays the tough guy, but if a real tough guy entered the picture, he'd grab his ankles like he was back in the shower room in jail."

There was a stunned moment of silence.

"You serious?" Ross said.

"Trust me. There's nothing there. Nothing."

Ross returned to the office the next day. For the next two weeks, Johnny called daily and threatened Ross. Each time he called, Ross told Johnny that he wasn't going to pay him. Not then, not ever. He said Johnny had made enough off of Ross, and that they were square. Then Johnny would erupt in a fountain of expletives. He really wasn't a creative a guy. The daily phone call became a ritual that marked the passing of every day. Then, without warning, the phone calls stopped. We don't know if Johnny gave up, was arrested, or was made to "disappear" by stronger, more dangerous men, but we never heard from him again.

I wish I could say that the Johnny experience ended our incursions into gambling, but that's a moral that only suits fairy tales and parables. Real life doesn't exactly work that way. Real life just continues to throw obstacles into your face until you overcome them or break down. In this incident, we just sidestepped the problem. Or the problem sidestepped us. Either way, we got lucky. But luck has a way of running out on you when you least expect it.

Ask any gambler.

Chapter Six

In 1990, Ross and I discovered a potentially lucrative new industry: electronic transaction processing. At this time, businesses were still accepting credit cards without the use of an electronic terminal. You may remember the old hand processing terminals: clerks would take your card, place it on a metal device, and run the slide bar over your credit card to make an impression on the receipt. The customer received the carbon copy, and the merchant kept the original for his records. At the end of the week (or month), the merchant would then take his credit card receipts to the bank in order to receive his payment.

Credit cards have been around as early as the 1920s when automobile owners used such cards to purchase fuel, and later evolved as a means for consumers paying merchants in the 1950s. The Diners Club card is generally considered the first general purpose charge card, soon followed by American Express. Visa came into being in the mid-1960s. The proliferation of credit cards can be attributed to capitalist-minded businesses that realized consumers were more apt to spend more money using credit cards than if paying for items with cash. Consumers enjoyed the freedom of being able to travel anywhere in the U.S. with a credit card and know that they possessed the power to purchase anything that they desired.

While innovative at the time, manual credit card machines proved to be more for the consumers' convenience of shopping quickly rather than the merchants' record keeping. After all, if the merchant should lose or misplace receipts, they suffered the financial loss. Furthermore, merchants had to make weekly bank deposits to receive payment, which was a time consuming process. If the business was small, this entailed the merchant closing down shop, and in turn, losing prospective sales opportunities.

However, electronic processing eliminated these shortcomings and ensured that the funds charged were directly deposited into the merchant's accounts. The old paper method was gradually being phased out as the technology boom of the early 1990s infiltrated its way into all segments of society. It was the perfect time to get in at the ground level of a fast-moving enterprise. After all, manual processing cost double (5%) what it cost to process credit cards electronically (2.5%). You didn't need to be Adam Smith to see the benefits afforded to the commercial sector by leveraging the benefits of advanced technologies. It was the way of the future, and Ross and I were going to ride the cusp.

We were approached by a man who sold the new electronic terminals for credit transactions. He was an older man, a good seller with a good pitch, simple, direct, and to the point. Sitting down over coffee at a local diner, he laid it on the table. If our company notified him of potential clients, we'd receive a cut of the profit if the client purchased a terminal.

At first, Ross and I had our doubts over whether or not the U.S. public would take to this revolutionary transaction process. From our experience, change was the one difficult product to sell to a mass market. People generally were resistant to it unless they saw some immediate benefit. Otherwise, they generally didn't like to rock the boat. Ross and I debated whether this new form of commerce would really generate interest in the business world. Instant commerce was a radical idea at the time. It sounded complicated, and, as we knew, people avoided unnecessary complication like the plague. Then there was the cost involved. The new terminals were expensive, and we were unsure if merchants would invest a couple grand for a terminal in addition to committing to a monthly service charge of fifty dollars or more, when they could just as easily continue with doing business in the status quo.

The offer sounded promising, but we ultimately declined. Still, the idea was intriguing enough to encourage Ross to research this growing industry. While change was difficult to implement to a reluctant audience, if valid, it was something that would take root and manifest regardless of public opinion. The willingness to embrace change and to implement it is what separated the Donald Trumps of the world from those wanting to be like Donald who never had the guts to lay it on the line. There was a reason why the names Thomas Edison, Henry Ford, Marie Curie, and of course Benjamin Franklin, to name a few, are held with sanctified awe; they were people that possessed unborrowed vision, who pushed forward despite contrary opinion, and who ultimately triumphed in the face of skepticism and adversity.

The more intrigued Ross became the more in depth he plunged into unfamiliar territory. He researched ceaselessly, immersing himself in the public library, making phone calls, and pouring over stacks of literature on the subject. The cellular industry he reasoned was become increasingly more competitive with the larger, more established companies steadily swallowing up or choking out the smaller ones. In the end, Ross understood that business was about adapting for long-term survival, to be ready to improvise to the commercial client, and be prepared to shift focus when the opportunity presented itself. Ultimately, Ross recognized that electronic processing promised the same level of potential as the cellular industry had promised just a few years prior. And with this realization, he decided to make his move, switching our company's direction away from cellular telecommunications to credit card terminals. He once again proved that a high school graduate with ambition and a keen eye for market sense didn't need business school to be successful. Over the next six months, Ross organized and launched a second business, A&R Bankcard.

We dissolved A&R Cellular and moved full force into the electronic processing arena. Ross quickly shared with me all of the nuances about the industry. I was charged with managing the daily operations of the company, while Ross concentrated on seeking out and establishing new contacts and clients. Initially, A&R Bankcard consisted of just Ross and me, as well as a receptionist, Valerie. Although it seemed that we had started back at square one, the excitement of striking out on a new venture and the possible rewards that lay before us made up for the difficult beginning. Again, twelve hour days became a part of our daily routine, essential for the success of a fledgling business. I had learned from my experiences with A&R Cellular that if you weren't committed to the company, the company would fail. And since failure wasn't an option for the Franklin brothers, twelve hours seemed like a paltry sacrifice to make to lead the kind of lifestyles we wanted so desperately for ourselves. Fortunately, electronic processing was not a hard sale to businesses. As computers became more commonplace, and information technology solutions proved cost-efficient and reliable, what once would have frightened off businesses was now becoming a necessity.

This time was a period of tremendous trial-and-error. While our business model essentially remained intact, we were still trying to determine the best ways to exploit a basically newfound industry. Hard work is always beneficial; however, it does not always make up for institutional knowledge that comes with ingrained experience. For example, at the onset, we were primarily concerned with the one-time commission earned for the lease or sale of the electronic processing equipment. Only later did we realize the potential income we could generate from recurring revenues. But at the time, A&R Bankcard was growing, and with its growth we added more employees to our company roster.

On paper, A&R Bankcard was an Independent Sales Organization (ISO), which is a term used for businesses in our industry. An ISO is a third party company that is contracted by banks to go out and solicit potential business clients for credit card servicing. An ISO signs up businesses to their service and then provides electornic processors to conduct merchant transactions. Often the ISO is responsible for maintaining customer service with the merchants throughout the duration of the contract, in the form of technical support.

Each month we generated about one hundred new accounts, an impressive number of additions to our inexperienced merchant portfolio. Still, relying on the acquisition of new clients is a risky practice; so much depended on a talented and aggressive sales force. Thus, as before with A&R Cellular, our sales force was the instrumental cog in the machine. At any given time, our sales team consisted of five to ten people, which was led by Lou James. Lou was a seasoned veteran salesman. A middle-aged man with graying hair, Lou maintained a confident but friendly disposition that is so crucial in meeting and winning over potential clients. He had that innate ability to size up customers at an instant and use the fluidity of language to play off their cautions and lure them in with a story and a smile. Lou's value was immeasurable, and while that was a benefit to A&R Bankcard, it was also a single point of failure. If he chose to leave us, it would impact our company significantly, and our productivity would plummet. Ross and I knew that in order to protect ourselves and the health of the company, we needed to secure more salespeople. We pooled our resources and hired three telemarketers and five aggressive salesmen to bolster the team.

The larger sales force proved difficult to manage. While we encouraged a laid-back atmosphere, there were those that mistook "relaxed" for comatose, and still others that pushed the limits of creative salesmanship. Ross and I understood that without a firm hand to guide the sales team, it would implode under misdirection and under-utilization. Since Ross was the front man glad-handing and keeping our name in the public eye, and I was securing ad space and running the administrative tasks of the office, the acquisition of an experienced manager was essential to keeping the sales team running at peak efficiency. After culling through an assortment of resumes, we ranked our applicants and scheduled them to come in for an interview at a fast-paced, fun, and rewarding company.

The moment Phil Jones came into our office, both Ross and I believed we had found our man. Phil's resume boasted a long list of managerial experience. He fancied himself a hired gun, a modern-day iteration of a problem-solver, taking jobs at places that were sorely in need of someone to set the tone and pace, creating order out of chaos, before leaving to find another desperate company in need of his services.

Phil was an affable man in his forties, the kind of person that was more comfortable in khaki pants than a business suit. He knew when to joke and when to sit quietly; he looked you directly in the eye as you spoke, nodding only to punctuate that he understood what you were saying. Phil related his previous experiences with sales staffs like ours and explained in detail how he corrected their errors and righted them on course. When he left, Ross and I were convinced we found the right man.

We were wrong.

At first, Phil patrolled the floors like a sociable shop foreman, politely shoulder surfing the sales staff, nodding in approval when good pitches were made and offering suggestions when the occasion warranted them. However, soon after, we began to notice changes in Phil's behavior. His time on the floor gradually dissipated, spending more time behind his closed office door than improving the commercial interaction with prospective clientele. Closed doors were a highly irregular sight at the office; my brother and I had long fostered an "open door" policy with closed offices a signal to the staff that important dialogue was transpiring. While we didn't think much of it at first, the next quarter sales figures started to cultivate my brother's and my suspicions. The next quarter was no different, with an even sharper decline in numbers. There were days when Phil would show up late or call in sick, which were becoming a frequent occurrence. The next time Phil came in, his eyes were bloodshot, he moved at a slow pace, and took ten aspirins over the course of six hours. Worse, Phil's dereliction of his responsibilities forced me to do his job. More than once I had to remind Phil on how to handle certain issues, and those days when he didn't show up at all, I had to assume the manager role in addition to my corporate responsibilities. I started to develop this gnawing feeling that I just couldn't shake. Booze, drugs, something was contributing to Phil's negligence. On the down low, I discreetly inquired about Phil among the sales team. Each time, I received similar feedback: slurred speech, smelling of alcohol, stumbling when he walked. The more I heard, the more I suspected Phil of being an alcoholic. When Chris, another member of the sales team, approached me in my office, it confirmed everything.

"I think Phil has a drinking problem," he said to me.

"I think so too. What happened?"

"When I walked into Phil's office just now, I thought I was going to get drunk off the fumes in there."

"That bad?" I asked.

"I think I caught him the other day adding something to his coffee. When I walked in his office, he was startled. He slammed one of the drawers quickly and yelled at me for not knocking. Thing is, I knocked three times, and he never said anything."

I sat back in my chair and ran my hand through my hair. It was pretty bad if Phil was drinking at the office, not to mention the potential law suits that could hit the company if something happened to anyone while he was under the influence.

"He has a bottle of Wild Turkey in his second drawer. I saw it. I went back later when he was at lunch, and it was right there plain as day."

I thanked Chris for the information and went to see my brother in his office.

"We got a problem," I said to him.

Ross was going through some paperwork. He looked up at me for a second then resumed what he was doing.

"When sales are down there's always a problem," he said. "I'll talk to him."

"He's an alky, Ross," I said.

"What?"

"He's a candidate for Betty Ford. I just talked to Chris. When people eat eggs for breakfast, this guy is swilling Kentucky's finest."

Ross paused. "What do you suggest?"

"He's a nice guy. But you know the expression."

"Yeah, nice guys finish lunch."

"And then they're fired," I added. "Bottom line is we can't afford to have the company's reputation tarnished because of him. His continued affiliation with us will only hurt in the long run."

"So let's show him the door."

Ross and I confronted Phil in his office. He was surprised to see us standing in front of him. Any time the owners come to you in your office it can only mean two things: a step up or a step out.

Phil denied it at first. He blustered angrily, telling us that the sales team was blaming him for their ineptness. When I opened his drawer and saw the bottle, his indignant act immediately deflated. He melted down to jelly. He told us about his problems, his lack of a social life, his debt. He said he'd get help. It was a sad state of affairs, really. Here was a guy so much older than us, with so much experience, practically crying to keep his job.

In the end, we let him go. Ross and I watched him pack up his stuff and escorted him to the front door. Phil kept his head down the entire time, avoiding all possible eye contact with the office. Truth be told, I felt sorry for Phil. We all had high hopes for him when he joined A&R Bankcard. But in a business that is fighting to earn its way in the industry, early setbacks can be devastating. And if you weren't going to succeed, you sure as hell didn't want it to be because of something that you should have corrected when you had the chance. We never saw Phil again. I hope he sought out the help he so desperately needed, but people can be hard-headed that way. Some need to split their heads open before they realize they're running into a brick wall. Phil was that kind of person.

They say bad luck comes in threes, and while I can't confirm the veracity of that statement, A&R suffered another setback shortly after the Phil fiasco. It is now and will be forever known as "the great receptionist rotation." In starting up a new business, sometimes things slip through the cracks. In our case, we hadn't installed an automated answering service yet, which meant that the receptionist had to be alert and answer every call and know who and how to transfer the caller to the appropriate contact person. If that person was out, she had to be able to take down accurate messages and make sure the person received them the moment they entered the office.

Valerie was our first receptionist and ended up being the one that lasted longer than all the ones following. She was a pleasant person with a friendly way about her, the kind of receptionist you want to handle heavy phone traffic. She could be polite or firm, depending on the situation. Although we didn't think much about it at the time, the submission of her resignation started a six-month merry-go-round of inept and downright useless replacements. Betty was the next candidate. She was strikingly attractive, with long straight black hair and a body that had been forged through endless repetition of aerobics workouts. The thing about Betty is that she couldn't handle the phone responsibilities. That first morning she accidentally hung up on customers, transferred calls to the wrong people, and couldn't type to save her life. She went out to lunch and never returned. Stephanie was our third hire. She was cute, not in the same category as Betty, but she had a way about her that you immediately liked. She could flirt with her eyes just right. Unlike Betty, she could actually meet the requirements of a receptionist. It was a short-lived breath of fresh air because Stephanie quit after only a month. She had decided to go back to school to become a teacher or something like that. I can't blame her. A receptionist is the kind of occupation you have to love or else it's just a temporary position, a way to make money until something better comes along. The depression that afflicted the predominantly male sales staff with Stephanie's departure was soon acquiesced by the hiring of Lori. If Betty was a ten on the beauty scale, then Lori was the mold from which the scale was created. Simply said, Lori turned heads wherever she went. She was a former Dallas Cowboys cheerleader that found her way to our front doors soon after she left

America's favorite football team. She was the kind of girl you'd break your neck trying to look at as you drove past her on the sidewalk. She had long blonde hair, a body you could bounce a quarter off of, and crisp blue eyes as if God himself had melted glacier ice and poured them Himself into her corneas. However, Lori wasn't long for the A&R world. The frenzied pace of multiple calls proved too much for her, and she soon left us after two short weeks to rejoin the Dallas Cowboys sidelines. At this point, Ross and I realized that we had to do some upgrading in the technology department. Good help was not only hard to find, it was becoming nearly impossible.

With the installation of an automated phone system, A&R Bankcard had reached another milestone in legitimizing itself as a future electronic transmission industry contender. Nevertheless, the equipment investment took a significant bite out of our operational budget, and in order to cut unnecessary costs, I decided to try my hand at the electrical trade since there were insufficient funds left to hire professional installers. It wasn't the prettiest job ever done, but like anything in life, you never know what you can do until you plod forward in the direction you want to go. At the end of the day, things worked. That's what mattered. It took us a full week to figure out exactly how to use the system, but that's another story.

When we pulled into the parking lot of the local golf course that afternoon, Lynn turned to me and groaned. She wasn't expecting this to be where our next "competition" would transpire, and it was painfully evident that as good as she was at pool, she was deficient in the world's greatest game.

"Golf? You must be kidding," she said.

"Balls. Holes. Sticks. It's just like pool only better."

"The green on the table is a bit shorter and without sand or water bordering it," she countered.

"I thought you wanted competition? If you want training wheels, we can go to putt-putt. The fairways are straighter, and the greens don't have any vicious, unseen breaks to them. Hey, it's cool either way. Just admit now that you can't handle a grown-up game." My teasing worked, because Lynn playfully but indignantly leapt out of the car.

"Okay, buster. You asked for it. I'm a quick study." With that she slammed the car door shut.

Lynn, in a word, sucked. Like so many who pick up the driver for the first time, she fell into the same traps of countless before her – she did not set her feet right, she swung too hard, trying to kill the ball off of the tee instead of guiding it, and she lifted her head before she struck the ball. On the fifth tee, she swung so hard, she nearly sent herself tumbling to the ground, eliciting a hearty chuckle from me.

"Sure, make fun of a girl," she teased, although there was a hint of resentment in her tonal inflection.

"Sorry, I just never saw a human tornado before," I laughed.

"Funny," she said. "This game sucks!" I could tell she was seriously contemplating flinging her driver into the fairway.

"You get no argument from me," I said. "Just ask any golfer. Doesn't matter if he's a weekend hack or PGA's finest. They'll both tell you the same thing."

"And what pray tell is that?"

"That allure lies in mastering the difficulties involved."

"That's deep," she huffed. "So why play the game? I mean really. If it takes someone countless years to develop it, what's the value in starting in the first place?"

I shrugged. "The clink."

"The clink?"

"The sound made when the club face and the ball connect at exactly the right spot," I explained. "You get 'the clink' and it will change your entire world."

Lynn squinted at me. She started pantomiming sliding on hip waders.

"What are you doing?"

"Putting on hip waders for the B.S. spilling out of your mouth."

I laughed.

"Seriously," I said. "Golf is a never-ending challenge that has torn up many a person's life. Even Tiger Woods didn't feel 'the clink' the first time his father set a club into his hands. But what keeps us coming out here is that second when you've struck the ball as perfectly as nature allows. There's magic in that moment where for one fleeting instant everything is in perfect alignment: form, swing, connection. Clink."

"Clink," she said again.

"Try it."

Lynn groaned, but despite making a half-assed effort like so may other girls would have done in this situation, I could tell she was taking the lessons I was trying to impart to her to heart. She carefully set her feet properly, her eyes fixed in a deep-rooted concentration. She measured and readjusted her grip. Then, when she was ready, she slowly drew back the club, slowly and deliberately. After a few seconds of mental preparation, she pulled the trigger, only this time the downswing was unhurried, allowing the club to build up speed according to the laws of physics. She kept her head down, watching the club face strike the ball.

It wasn't a "clink," but she hit the ball straighter than she had all day. The only thing was that it landed into a bunker a hundred and fifty yards away.

"Great," she said. "Got any words of wisdom for hitting out of a sand trap?"

"There are just so many hours in a day."

As was her habit in these situations, Lynn slapped me playfully on the arm. Touching was a good sign. It means that a connection wants to be made.

"Come on," I said before any awkwardness set in. "Time to practice your pitching wedge."

Lynn's first outing was akin to many first-timers' experiences: generally bad, but with enough good moments to keep her interested in rectifying what was going wrong. And in that she finally understood the allure of the game. This is what I liked about her. She never got so frustrated with her performance that she wanted to call it quits; when she flubbed a shot, she asked me where she went wrong and tried not to repeat the mistake a second time. This was easier on some shots than others, but if she made a particularly bad one, she insisted on trying it a second or third time so that she grasped the mechanics behind the swing for that particular situation. When a person displays passion for something, it's infectious.

Clearly, she saw my love of the game, how I reveled in every act whether it be setting the ball properly on the tee, or recalculating the breaks on a green, and it rubbed off on her. In turn, instructing her and then watching her implement the lesson made me feel closer to her. We were out there for hours, but the afternoon seemed to breeze by in a matter of minutes.

After our game, I took her to an early dinner and an ice cream cone. Over the course of the day, we exchanged little personal details and life stories. I told her of Ross's and my company, how we started with literally nothing but had overcome early setbacks through a combination of hard work, perseverance, and a lot of luck. She told me about her life and the series of events that brought her to Texas. I hung onto every word she said, voracious to know the minutest detail that would somehow give me a more profound insight into her likes and dislikes, where she came from, and where she was now headed.

"For the longest time I wanted to be a painter," she said as I walked her to the front of her apartment building. "So I just up and quit my job."

"Just like that?" I said. "Gutsy."

She licked the vanilla ice cream off her hand where it had melted down off the cone.

"What better way to become a painter than to actually paint?"

"So young and yet so wise," I said.

Lynn smiled, and I matched hers with my own. We held that moment a bit too long, and first-date awkwardness settled in. Nothing is worse than running out of conversation right at the moment when you know the date is coming to its conclusion and you weren't sure whether you should kiss the girl, or act like a gentlemen in the hope that a second date was right around the corner.

"I had a good time," I said when all other words failed me.

Lynn's dark eyes flashed, and a mischievous grin creased her lips.

"Oh? You always have a good time when you beat a girl?"

"Well, to be honest, I should have beaten you more in retaliation for the debacle at the pool table the other night."

"Oh yeah? So why didn't you?" There was that smirk again.

"I was distracted."

"By what?"

"By this…"

I have never been an aggressive kisser, typically allowing the girl to at least give me some subtle invitation, whether it was leaning in close as she talked, or touching my arm, or twirling her hair. But there are exceptions to every rule, and this was one of them. The first kiss is always memorable – good or bad – it sticks with you for a long time. I've found that urgency plus passion have been the necessary ingredients for the better ones. When I pressed my lips against hers, it was as a moment frozen in time that passed all too quickly. When the kiss ended, I was breathless and flushed.

"Can I call you tomorrow?" I asked.

"You know the number," she responded.

On my way back to the car, she called out to me.

"Adam."

I stopped and turned back to her. She had a serious look on her face.

"There's nothing wrong with making a buck – if that's what you really want."

This was a funny thing for her to say, and what I was thinking must have registered on my face.

"What makes you think I don't want it?"

"Rich kids don't shoot pool," she said.

"But they do golf, and I can crush the ball off the tee," I reminded her with a smile that made her smile too.

"G'night, Adam."

She blew me a kiss and closed the door. I stood there for a second, reveling in the breeze that had kicked up, which in my mind came more from her lips than the sun's influence on atmospheric pressure, which inevitably causes wind. I mean, really, which is more believable?

The one problem with sales, as anyone will tell you who's ever been involved in the business, is that there is always a high turnover. It's a high pressure field if you're a born salesman, and if you're not fortunate to have been born with the gift of talking paint off of a wall, it's about a hundred times more demanding. It's not uncommon for salesmen to get burned out. You work the phones and pound the pavement just to find customers. Then the hard part of making the sale begins. Some of these guys spend precious hours just to have the deal fall apart at the seams. When you work on commission, a dropped sale can make a difference when the mortgage is due.

Fortunately, Ross and I seemed to have a never-ending supply of bodies to fill the sporadic vacancies. The sales staff and middle management were quickly replaced with our friends that wanted the opportunity to achieve the success that Ross and I had. The hiring of our friends was a tremendous asset to A&R Bankcard for two reasons: one, all of the new employees, particularly the floor supervisors, allowed Ross and me to concentrate on our strategic sales plan, which is where we made our profit; and two, hiring our friends gave the company a homegrown, comfortable feel that had always been our goal. From day one, we had wanted to maintain a fun, friendly atmosphere in whatever enterprise we pursued. It was the hallmark of our first business, and while good fun shouldn't get in the way of working, it was pertinent to maintaining an employee-favorable environment. Work hard, play hard. It might come across as a cliché, but a company that was able to marry the two was always a successful one.

After a few rough spots, A&R Bankcard had entered its renaissance. Sales were up, profits were increasing, and everyone had more money in their pockets than ever before. Whoever said money was the root of all evil wasn't that far off. Extra money is an enabler; it facilitates whatever passion, whatever addiction you might have. If you like wine, you buy more expensive wine. If you like cars, you buy more expensive cars. And if you gamble, well, you're as good as hooked.

It was during this time when Ross and I had our second foray into gambling, and this one could have been potentially more costly than our run in with Johnny No-Balls. It all started with Bill Gardner. Bill was a business contact of ours who ran a printing company in Dallas. He was a down-to-earth Texan that ran his business in the same manner as if he were running an ice cream stand. No matter how relaxed he was, his work never suffered for it. If he didn't run his own company, he would have been the kind of person we would have recruited to work for us.

Every time we'd pick up our supplies from Bill, we'd chat about sports. He would tell us what games he betted on, how we did for the week, whether he was up or down for the season. The fact that he gambled wasn't lost on us. In fact, it merely solidified the friendship that we had already established. We swapped war stories, games that made or broke us, and how we blew the money.

A few days before the beginning of the professional football season, Ross and I were picking up some materials from Bill's office when he mentioned that he was going to Las Vegas for the opening weekend of the NFL.

"Vegas, man! That's going to be incredible!" Ross said.

"Best party in town. You should see the place when football starts. It's like Disneyland, only better."

"I bet some serious action is going down that weekend," I said.

"Only the Super Bowl beats it. The betting pit is jammed. They have to put more waitresses on call because there are so many people."

"Who are you picking?" Ross asked.

"My money's on Denver."

"Over the Cowboys? You could get lynched in this state for such a sacrilege," I said, laughing.

"Boys, my heart's Cowboys country, but I bleed green. Gamblers are fans of no teams."

"You got a point there," Ross agreed.

"You want me to place a bet down for you? There's no way Denver can lose."

Ross and I looked at each other. While we didn't gamble to the degree that we did before, we still kept our minds sharp. That summer when the NFL draft took place, we had spent countless hours debating teams' rankings. We figured quarterbacks' passing rates, team receptions, even the defense and special teams. We spent the better part of the weekend coming up with our own rankings and analysis. At the end of it all, there was one lone team on top: Denver.

"What do you think," Ross said to me. "We got the money."

Moments like this were so rare in the gambling world. It was as close to a sure thing as you can get. That afternoon, Ross delivered a suitcase with ten thousand dollars in it to Bill to place on the Denver Broncos. He told Bill to call us when he arrived in Vegas and found out what the line of the bet was.

The afternoon Bill would arrive in Vegas, Ross and I sat together at my apartment. Just like when we were kids, were dreaming of all the junk that we could already buy ourselves with the winnings.

Ross checked his watch.

"It's late. Shouldn't he have called us by now?" he asked.

I glanced at my own watch. It was nearly five o'clock.

"He was supposed to call us by four. Maybe he's held up. It is opening weekend. The betting pit must be mobbed."

"He better get his ass to a phone soon," Ross muttered.

We waited. And waited. Still, there was no call from Bill. Exhilaration gave way to anxiety, which gave way to anger, and then finally to concern.

"What if he got jacked?" Ross asked. "What if someone stole our money?"

"I'm sure he's fine. Probably got caught up in everything."

"If he is fine, he'd better have placed that bet."

"I'm sure he did. It was his idea, right? It's not like we asked for a favor."

"There's ten K in that briefcase," Ross said.

"What's your point?"

"Lots of reasons not to place the bet," Ross cryptically retorted.

"He wouldn't do that," I said. But still it got me thinking. "He better not have done that," I corrected myself. Gambling may be a kindred addiction, but it's certainly not the most honorable. Case and point: my brother and Johnny.

The next morning we got our call bright and early from Bill.

"Hey, guys. Sorry it's taken me so long to get in touch. I got distracted last night when I arrived. You know, Vegas and all. I'm on my way now to place the bet. Give me a few, and I'll call you back with the line."

Needless to say, we were very much relieved. After all, this was the most significant bet we had ever placed before. It might not make Donald Trump blink twice, but it made our hearts pitter-patter.

And I'd be lying if I didn't have just a twinge of guilt for thinking poorly of Bill the day before. But that changed when after an hour of waiting, we didn't receive our confirmation phone call.

Another hour passed. Ross and I sat in an angry silence. Ross got up and grabbed the phone.

"I'm going to call him."

He punched in the number and looked over at me with a stern face. Yeah, he was pissed. But so what? So was I. Our cash was somewhere in Vegas.

"Bill, it's Ross. We want to know if you placed the bet. Let us know."

Click! He hung up.

Another hour. No call. No ring. Nothing.

Ross called again.

And again.

And again.

All weekend we called, and still we heard nothing from Bill. Our friends thought we were complete suckers, a thought that must have crossed my mind at least a thousand times. Over and over we heard the same response: "What would possess you to give some guy ten grand in cash and send him off to Vegas?" And we couldn't get mad at the lack of sympathy. When you release a balloon from your hand, you have only one option left: you watch it go.

Monday afternoon, Bill finally got around to calling us at the office.

"Bill, where the hell are you!?" Ross demanded.

"Guys, I have some explaining to do, I know."

"Explaining? You better have a Shakespeare story to tell, Bill."

"Ask him where our money is," I said to Ross.

And so Bill told us. Apparently, when he was out in the City of Sin, he had taken the opportunity to use our money – the cash that we gave him – to settle some outstanding bills his company had accrued. He said that he hadn't intentionally used us to "loan" him the money, but he was caught between a rock and a hard place. Personally, I had a good idea of what I wanted to do with that rock.

Bill ended up paying us back our ten thousand dollars plus five hundred in interest the following week, but the return of the money did nothing to improve our moods. We felt incredibly foolish for the blind trust we bestowed upon Bill simply because he seemed like a good guy. Of course, our escapade provided fodder for the office jokes. Our friends had a limitless reservoir of gag material that they used in the office, on the basketball court, and in the bars. Although it was in the spirit of good-natured fun, the teasing reminded Ross and me that we had made an incredibly naïve and immature decision. We were running a business and couldn't be careless. Being careless in our personal lives could easily translate into being reckless in our business lives. A serious lesson was learned.

To add insult to injury, Denver won the game and covered the spread. If Bill had placed our bet, we would have doubled our money.

Chapter Seven

One of our most important long-term projects at A&R involved increasing the number of our direct salespeople while at the same time winnowing out the external sales agents we were employing in a contract capacity. This was an especially critical process as up until the reorganization, external agents had been our bread and butter. However, developing a capable and highly qualified in-house staff was necessary to give legitimacy to the company, as well as wean A&R off its reliance on an external sales force. In the past, external agents had proven a powerful asset, but they had a tendency to be less communicative and responsive to our input. Exacerbating the matter was that these agents were more likely to drop unforeseen problems in our laps and were less prone to go the extra mile as they didn't have any financial investment at stake. Complicating the situation was the ever-present reality that these hired guns could sling their talents elsewhere, namely competitors, at any moment.

One external agent in particular caused us considerable grief: Paul. He was a fairly successful salesman, and he approached Ross about improving his sales. At first we thought Paul was a go-getter, a person always seeking to gain the edge on his profession, a true forward thinker. Ross sat down and talked to him, and together they struck a deal: Paul would hire a sales team to work directly under his supervision, and A&R would train them for him. As Paul's new team learned the business, they would send more clients our way. It seemed like a mutually-beneficial arrangement.

Paul's work ethic was never a problem; rather, he possessed what I can best describe as an unsavory personality. For one, he was an unabashed teller of tales with the ability to stretch the limits of the truth to suit his needs. He was so extravagant that he made Billy look like an amateur. It was never a big trout he caught, but a fifteen foot shark. He didn't see a celebrity at a restaurant; he sat down and had dinner with her. And if that wasn't bad enough, Paul was a chatty Cathy. He would call the office several times a day (his personal record was fifteen calls over the course of eight hours) just to make small talk. He'd always end up getting transferred to either Ross's or my phone line, and he'd end up talking about a tire sale or some inane commercial that he saw on television the previous night. Thirdly, after our experience with Frank, there were signs and indications that Paul was someone who hit the sauce and hit it hard.

My suspicions about Paul's excessive alcohol use were confirmed one afternoon at a training event. Paul had asked us to organize a workshop for some of his new salespeople, and, per our agreement, we complied. At eight o'clock sharp, everyone was sitting in their seats waiting for the dog-and-pony show, everyone that is except Paul. He was late. Correction, he was *very* late. After an hour, he rolled into the conference room where we had begun the first part of the workshop reeking unmistakably of cheap tequila. The stink was enough to draw stern stares from some of the new employees. Paul did his best to play it straight, but Visine can only do so much to reduce the glare of bloodshot eyes, and even if you swallow a whole tube of Crest, the acrimonious odor of a ten-dollar bottle of tequila is going to penetrate fluoride and mouthwash.

I continued on with the training session, all the while devising a strategy as how to best handle the situation. Paul was a good earner, but keeping someone on the payroll with a chemical dependence is a slippery slope. The numbers might hold in the short-term, but it was only a matter of time before the addiction got the best of a person. The more I thought about this, the angrier I became. Ross and I would later joke about how we were magnets for drunks, but at the time I was more concerned with keeping the company moving in a forward trajectory. After all, who did Paul think he was? I could see Paul nodding off from time to time, his head bobbing in that interlude before sleep overwhelms a person. To put it mildly, I was pissed.

At the conclusion of the training, I didn't acknowledge him, even when he came over to me by the coffee and donut table. I left him standing there looking bewildered, his shirt incorrectly buttoned, his shirt tail hanging down the front of his jeans.

I didn't miss a beat. I headed straight into Ross's office, slamming the door behind me.

"We got another one," I said, plopping down in the chair in front of my brother's desk.

"Another what?"

"Paul. He showed up to the training session three sheets to the wind."

"You're kidding."

I pointed to my mouth. "You don't see me smiling, do you?"

Ross let out a groan. "What are we, a half-way house for drunken salespeople?"

"He's got to go."

Ross sat there a few seconds mulling it over.

"He makes us a lot of money," he said finally.

"Ross," I pressed. "I've got three words: liability, liability, liability."

It took us ten minutes to reach a decision: Paul had to go. While we may have been young men in charge of a thriving company, the last thing we needed was for our competition – people with cutthroat experience – to think we were running our business like a frat house. If they smelled a weakness, they were going to exploit it. And we couldn't let that happen.

We passed the word in the office that Paul was never to be allowed entrance. The next morning, I contacted Paul personally to inform him that he was barred from the office. Paul's indignation on the phone was almost comical. He sounded like a six-year-old girl whose mother told her she can't have a cookie before dinner.

"Paul, we just can't have that kind of behavior going on. It's unacceptable."

"I know. It was just one time. I swear."

"Did you see the looks some of the new employees were giving you? How do you expect to be a leader when your team won't respect you?"

"I understand. Really I do. It was just one time. An old friend came into town, and we went out and things got kind of out of hand. Then we saw that backup running back from the Cowboys, and one thing led to another, and next thing I know shots were being handed out."

Even though I was skeptical of the story, I told Paul that we were still interested in doing business with him. As Ross pointed out, Paul's team was gaining momentum, and we had invested substantial time and energy in their training. It would be bad business to sever a successful business relationship because of personalities.

I explained to him that instead of him bringing contracts to our office directly, he was to either mail them to us or slip them under the front door. Paul didn't mask his tone of disappointment or the fact that he was put off that he could no longer step foot on our property, which meant he could not attend the training of his own sales force. That was the deal, I told him. Take it or leave it. He took it.

A few days later, the receptionist called me to let me know that Paul was at the front door wanting to come into the office.

"He's literally begging me to let him in," she explained. "It's kind of creepy in a way."

I headed up to the front where Paul was standing, his right hand clutching a manila file folder and his left palm spread across the glass door. He appeared as if he had slept in his clothes; his shirt was rumpled and un-tucked, and there was a stain of God-knows-what down the left thigh of his pants. His hair, typically combed to perfection, was unruly with large tufts going this way and that. He was a mess.

When he saw me, Paul mouthed the word "please" long and slow like a child who's begging his father to let him stay up and watch the late game. It was truly a pathetic, and dare I say, comical site.

So much so that I bit my lower lip to hold back my laughter. I wanted to give him a juice box or something. One, because he looked like he really needed the fluids, and two, because he was so kid-like that only something silly like a juice box fit the humor of the moment.

But I didn't do anything. I didn't buckle and let him. I merely gave him a dispassionate look, then turned on my heels and went back into my office. My receptionist told me later that Paul stood out there for a half-hour before slipping the folder under the door and walking dejectedly back to his car. He never pulled another stunt like that again. I often wondered how he felt about what he'd done when he'd come off his bender, or if he had any recollection of the incident at all. When you run a company, you meet all sorts of people with all sorts of idiosyncrasies and problems. I imagine it's very similar to tending to a flock of sheep. Some stay in line, and some stray. Paul was one who strayed. Who knows? Maybe the wolves got him. Or the bottle. In the end, it's the same result.

I was supposed to take Lynn out to a nice dinner on our second date, but I ended up having to cancel at the last minute because of work. To complicate matters, I had to cancel on her a second time, a fact that did not set well with her. We had talked a few times on the phone since our first date, chatting non-stop until the first rays of the sun would creep up over the horizon. It was like high school again, when talking to someone you liked on the phone took precedence over food, drink, bathroom, or sleep. It was like that with Lynn; time passed without notice. The more we shared about our lives with each other, the more we wanted to know. It was like trying to feed an insatiable hunger with sustenance that served only to dull the sharpness of the wanting.

When she said that I could make it up to her on the golf course, I actually felt my heart skip a beat. If you had told me five years ago that I would not only find a beautiful woman that would be interested in me, but also one that actually wanted to share my interests, I would have bet the farm that you were crazy. Yet here I was, not only forgiven for my absentminded blunder, but also asked to provide restitution in the place I revered as one of the holiest on earth! I was sitting in the proverbial catbird seat.

So I took Lynn to the driving range where I could start ironing out mistakes in her swing. It was a beautiful morning; the temperature had not begun its unbearable ascent; the die-hards were on the range with us practicing chip shots and drives; the sprinkler spun in the background, keeping the practice putting greens their deep emerald color.

Lynn showed me her driving stance.

"Feet at shoulder-width," I instructed. "Firm grip, but not too tight. You're not choking a snake. Face down. Eyes on the ball. That's it. You're burning worms out there because you're picking your head up on the downswing. Watch the club connect, then as you follow through, you can see where it's going."

"Burning worms?"

"Golf slang for those drives where the ball barely gets off the ground."

"Ha-ha."

"Swing already."

Lynn brought the driver down. The shot was better than her first dozen. The sound was loud and metallic; she missed the sweet spot, and the club reverberations must have been hell on her hands and forearms. Still, the ball took off, going straight before arcing to the right.

"You sliced it."

"Is that good or bad?"`

"It isn't pie, so no, it's not good."

"You're hysterical," Lynn said, smirking and giving me the finger.

"Look," I said. "I'm sorry about the other night. A work thing just popped up. Ross was losing his head, and when he gets like that, it's easier just to stay with him until he works it out. Turned out to be nothing major, but you couldn't tell him that at the time. He's a bit obsessed."

"That's what you have to watch out for," she said, taking a practice swing.

"What do you mean?"

"Becoming obsessed. There's a difference between being driven to do something and being obsessed about doing something. It may be a fine line, but there is one."

"Didn't someone once say that obsession was just a healthy way of expressing yourself?"

Lynn frowned. My voice trailed off. Not funny.

"I understand when work obligations come up. Once is fine, but when you cancelled out twice, and for something that turned out not to be such a serious issue, that's when red flags are raised."

"Red flags?"

"You know what I'm talking about. I'm serious here, Adam. You're a nice guy, and I like you. But don't make this a habit, okay?"

My voice softened. "Ross is trying to make some big deals. I have to support him. He's not only my brother, Lynn. He's my partner. It's not exactly like I have a choice." It was a weak argument, and I immediately regretted letting it come out of my mouth the way it did. The simple fact was that I probably could have gotten out of the last work emergency; I just didn't have the heart to do it was all. I'd feel guilty knowing that Ross was in the office while I was out having a good dinner with a great girl.

"It's all about choices, Adam. From what you've said about him, your brother makes risky ones at times and drags you in for the ride. And what for? Money. Just money."

"Why does everyone who has come from money always say that? When you don't have a lot, and never did, it means something, Lynn. It makes the world go round."

"Money is a means not an end."

She was right. I softened.

"You're right, and I'm sorry. It's just – I've been working since I was sixteen. Growing up, my mother had barely two nickels to rub together. You know how hard it is to try to do homework when you see your mother leaving the house for her second job?"

"I'm sure it was difficult."

"It broke my heart. I promised myself then that I wouldn't be in that situation when I was older. Some times at night, my brother and I would lie in bed listening for the sound of her car pulling into the driveway. It would be two, three in the morning. And then she'd come into the house, and I'd hear her throw her keys on the kitchen table, before she dragged herself down the hall to her bedroom for three hours of sleep before she had to wake up and do it all over again."

I had never told anyone that. It was something Ross and I had kept between us, a secret between brothers. Not that we were embarrassed by it, mind you. Our mother had always been the source of our strength. But because it was private, I was reluctant to share it with just anyone. Standing there at the driving range, it seemed important to relate to Lynn who listened attentively, nodding her head in silent understanding.

"I admire you, Adam. I really do. What you've accomplished – what you continue to accomplish – is nothing short of amazing. I'm just concerned for you is all. I mean, businesses ebb and flow with the high and low times. What happens when you hit a rough patch?"

"Nothing like that is going to happen," I said.

"You say that now, but later? What are you going to do if things take a down turn? Are you going to self-destruct? Do you see what I'm saying? You're riding high now, but what will you do – how will you react – when things aren't going your way?"

To be honest, the thought had never entered my mind. My goal, as well as Ross's, was to make it, pure and simple. To become successful and retire in our thirties and do whatever those successful people did with their time. After the company got up and running, never once had I considered the possibilities of us not obtaining that goal. There were some doubts in the beginning, but Ross had shown me what could be and what could happen. And once that pill was swallowed, success was an inherent right, not something that had to be earned. It seemed beyond reason that this could happen, something so incalculable that it was futile to even consider the consequences.

"I don't know... play golf?"

For the second time that day, Lynn frowned. She replaced the club in her bag and walked off the driving range toward the club house. It was our first fight.

Our office was always looking for ways to break up the monotony of the average workday, and it should come as little surprise that gambling became one of our preferred pastimes. We would make small wagers on just about anything, betting ten bucks that the receptionist would wear her plunging neckline red shirt that day, or five bucks that we could get back from lunch in twenty minutes, things like that. It was juvenile antics to be sure, but the little things go a long way, and we were always trying to balance out the demanding routines of business with ways to keep up office morale.

In Texas, there are a few items of interest indigenous to the state. There is high school football, oil companies, and large ranches, but there is also Tex-Mex food. Texas must have more fast food "authentic" Tex-Mex establishments all heralding their expertise in the fine arts of enchiladas, tacos, and of course, refried beans. One day, a group of us ended up discussing the pros and cons of refried beans, the merits of their taste and nourishment value. As the conversation snow balled, one of the sales staff, Ben, bragged that he could eat, single handedly, two quarts of refried beans.

When someone makes a statement like that, you have two choices: either raise his bet, or call him on it. Ross, never having been a big fan of Ben's, called him on it.

"Bullshit," Ross said.

"I'm telling you the truth," Ben said.

"Do you even know how many beans are in two quarts?"

"Hey, if they're good, they're good."

"You'd explode first," I said, laughing. I could only imagine the after effects of eating two quarts of a substance that basically made you fart for hours afterwards.

"How much?" Ross said.

"How much, what?"

"Put your money where your mouth is, Pancho Villa. I bet you fifty bucks you can't eat two quarts of refried beans."

"I'll cover that bet," Ben said. "Now if we only had some…"

"Oh, we can get them."

Ross called in our receptionist and asked her to bring us back two quarts of refried beans when she got back from lunch. She made a face when we explained to her the wager at stake. She wrinkled her nose and told us we were gross.

The staff waited around the conference table. Side bets were being placed, and of course, the good-natured ribbing continued over the next hour. Ben bathed in the attention, laughing and making flatulence noises until the receptionist returned with two quarts of beans. The time had arrived.

Ben poked the plastic spoon through its wrapper and opened the first quart to his right. He looked up at Ross.

"Ready?" he inquired of my brother.

"Whenever you are," Ross responded.

Ben started spooning the beans into his mouth at a steady pace. The rest of us sat there eating our lunches while we watched him. It was like watching a poor man's gladiatorial event. The fighter against the beans. Who would win?

Spoonful after spoonful went into Ben's mouth. At first, there was nothing but pleasure in his eyes and face. But after the tenth helping, Ben's face began to show signs of wear and tear. I looked at the beans. They were a little burnt and dry. They had to feel like concrete mix in his mouth. But Ben kept plodding along. After he d eaten about half of the first quart, Ben began to shift in his seat uneasily. And then it happened. The first of a long line of wet sounding farts escaped him.

"Gross!" someone shouted.

"There's more where that came from," Ben said.

He finished the first quart in about twenty minutes, pushing the empty container toward the center of the table. I looked around the room and saw the majority of the spectators brave enough to still remain in the room holding paper towels over their noses. The air in the room was quite ripe.

"You ready to give in yet?" Ross asked him.

"I'm just getting started," Ben replied, accenting his response with a long, drawn out fart.

He started in on the second quart. After the third spoonful, Ben's face suddenly changed. To this day, I will swear that I heard some deep growl in his stomach. It sounded like someone opening a rusty metal door. Ben's eyes got wide with fear. This wasn't natural.

Chants of "do it, do it" started to swell in the room.

In went another spoonful. Then another.

I heard that noise again and looked at Ben. He had not only heard it, but felt it deep in the recesses of his bowel.

And then after the fifth helping of the second quart, Ben suddenly shot up from the table. His eyes were watering; his stomach was making primeval noises.

"Ben! Ben! Ben!" chanted the peanut gallery.

And in the midst of all that ceremony and pomp, Ben barely grabbed the tin trashcan in time to catch a powerful stream of brown vomit that exploded from his mouth like a broken sewer pipe. I don't remember how many times he expelled refried beans from his stomach, but when he was finally done, when he lifted his head up from the trashcan, his eyes were watery, and saliva ran from his mouth like the drool of a St. Barnard. He looked like he had just given birth.

Ross had no pity. He slapped Ben on the back and brought the remaining carton of refried beans to him.

"You want some more?"

Ben had a downright pitiful look on his face. But much to his credit, he didn't complain or say a word. He just fished out a Ulysses S. Grant from his pants, handed it to Ross, and exited the conference room. He spent the better part of the afternoon with Pepto Bismo in the bathroom. He was the butt of jokes for the next two weeks, but he took his punishment like a man. In the end, the refried beans proved an insurmountable feat. He didn't eat them again for six months.

Chapter Eight

That year, the fantasy football crazy swept through our office, and Ross, me, and several of our friends formed a league. Fantasy football was a natural progression for people who loved sports and betting, and not necessarily in that order. Fantasy football fed our competitive spirits as well as provided an outlet for trash-talking and taunting. There was no greater humiliation than to suffer an embarrassing loss and have to hear about it for five full days.

As fantasy folklore would have it, the fantasy football phenomenon was first conceived in 1962 by three founding members in a New York City hotel room. Interest in the game of professional football itself was waning. The nation at the time was caught somewhere in the middle of the Cuban Missile Crisis, and the threat of nuclear war was at its most pronounced height. So these three visionaries sat down over drinks and started to draft what would be the framework of the fantasy football we know today, drawing up rules, procedures, and of course, the most entertaining part of it all, the actual players' draft. The Greater Oakland Professional Pigskin Prognosticators League (GOPPPL) was conceived in 1963. As was so eloquently stated in the league's charter, "The purpose of this league is to bring together some of Oakland's finest Saturday morning gridiron forecasters to pit their respective brains (and cash) against each other." Forty-seven years later, what started off as a "good idea" has blossomed into a multi-billion dollar business.

Not surprisingly, Ross especially liked fantasy football and took his team more seriously than Jerry Jones took the Cowboys. Ross was constantly working trades, trying to assemble the greatest team in the history of fantasy football. He was borderline cutthroat and was not afraid to use his power of persuasion to pressure less-than-eager friends to make unfavorable trades. My friends would often talk to me off-line to complain about Ross's dictatorial tactics. He would corner them in the break room or call them up at late hours in the hopes of finding them at a weak point and then like a jungle cat whose prey is cornered, attack their throat. Someone once said, "one complaint, and it's a personality issue; two complaints is a conspiracy; three complaints, there's a problem." Over the next few days I watched Ross work the phones, badgering people with his relentless style. I was almost appreciative of his style; he could switch his approach from a bully into a potential ally all within the scope of a conversation. And sure enough, one by one, Ross would finagle the best players from the other teams, whether through unwitting compliance or just dog-eared exhaustion of listening to one pitch after another. A running joke was that Ross should quit the credit card business and become the NFL Commissioner. I have little doubt that Ross had entertained that very thought on several occasions.

Partly out of sympathy to my fellow "coaches" and partly because Ross had secured himself firmly in first place, I decided to do something that would lessen the size of Ross's swelled head and arrogance. In order to fulfill my objective I enlisted the assistance of Robert, the recent victim of one of Ross's assaults, into my plan. It was simple. We would create a fake trade offer from another member of the league, something too good for any aggressive person to pass on. Once Ross took the bait, and the trade was on the table, we would pull the carpet from under Ross's feet, and we would then reveal ourselves as the perpetrators of the farce.

I asked Robert to create a bogus e-mail account and send the potential trade offer from it to Ross. No one knew my brother better than me; there was little chance of him noticing the e-mail address or questioning the validity of the unfamiliar account name.

Robert began sending e-mails to Ross as if he were Sam, another member of our league who had Emmitt Smith on his team. In the e-mail, Robert insinuated that Sam was interesting in trading

Smith to Ross in exchange for a pair of some good, but less than stellar players. The trade looked legit; "Sam" would fill two needs on his team in exchange for giving up a star player. It was a brilliant move. Ross was immediately excited at the prospect of adding the NFL's premiere running back, which in turn would solidify his team as the strongest in the league. At the time, Emmitt Smith was at the pinnacle of his career winning both a Super Bowl and League MVP award in the past season. As a lifelong Cowboys fan, Ross had long coveted Smith and tried every deal he could think of to acquire him. While Sam had refuted Ross's previous attempts, an apparent mutually equitable deal coupled with Sam's poor team standings gave the overture an aura of legitimacy. Secretly, Robert and I knew Ross would be chomping at the bit at the prospect of making this savvy coup. It was the perfect practical joke.

What made this scheme even more doable was the fact that Ross wasn't very computer literate. Despite his business success, computer skills were the one thing that eluded him. He had managed to bluff his way through any endeavor that required the use of a computer with his charm, and then he'd always ask me later to show him how to complete the task. For example, he rarely if ever sent any e-mail correspondence, preferring the time honored tradition of telephone calls. He always relied on me to handle the technical communications in all facets of our business. He just didn't embrace the technological revolution in his personal life, a shortcoming that I was eager to exploit.

The morning after Robert sent the first e-mail, I was in our office with Ross. At the time, we were still sharing office space with our friend Mac. The cramped quarters provided me a front row opportunity to see the gag's unfolding. As per his usual routine, Ross fiddled with the computer for a while shortly after arriving at work. I kept an eye on him as he scrolled through the night's correspondence. Suddenly, he sat upright in his chair and emitted a surprised giggle when he came upon the e-mail. He could hardly contain himself.

"What's up?" I asked him as he fidgeted in his chair.

"What? Oh, nothing. The usual crap," he said, hesitating before he answered. I could see the cogs in his head turning, a sign that he was already setting up his team for the week.

"You sure?" I pressed him, wondering if he would give up his golden goose.

"Yeah. Same old, same old."

I tried hard to fight back the urge to smile. He wasn't going to tell me about the trade offer, and I was trying to control giving him a signal that something was rotten in the state of Denmark. Ever the scrupulous businessman, Ross was going to hold onto that piece of information until the deal was set in stone. But deep down, I knew he wanted to announce to the world his conquest. It was eating him alive not to lord it over me and rub it in my face. I let him enjoy his little secret, knowing that I would have the final trump.

Later that afternoon, Robert popped into my office. His face was lit up brighter than a kid's on Christmas Day.

"It's working. Ross replied to my e-mail."

"What did he say?" I asked.

"He says he's interested, but he's trying to act coy. He wants Emmitt badly."

"You should have seen him this morning when he opened the e-mail. I thought he was going to piss his pants he was so excited."

"Did he say anything?"

"You know him. You couldn't have pried a pin out of his mouth with a tractor he was so tight-lipped. He's waiting to spring it when the deal's complete. He likes to strut around like a peacock."

"I can't wait to prune his feathers when we tell him it was a joke."

"We should have a camera for this."

Robert and I cracked up. It was rare that anyone ever got the better of Ross. When those times do happen, you always want to have a memento as a keepsake.

Over the next couple of days, Robert continued to string Ross along, playing the part of the nervous coach not really sure he wanted to trade his best player. I watched Ross the whole time, compulsively checking his e-mail account, pounding furiously on the keyboard when a response was required.

"Jesus, you hit those keys any harder, you're going to snap your fingers," I teased him.

"Welcome to the business world," he responded, not once looking up from the computer monitor.

"I think I've seen you check your e-mail more in the past three days then all of last year."

"Technology is our friend. I just want to stay on top of things."

"You need some help?"

"No!" he said, and when he realized he answered a little too fast, added, "I got it covered."

I just nodded my head. We'd see about that, I thought to myself.

The day before we had to set up our lineups for the weekend games, Ross was sitting in front of his computer. He had gotten there early that morning and hadn't left his seat. He didn't even say good morning to me when I walked through the door, his eyes glued to his e-mail inbox.

"Hey there, Ross," I said in an upbeat, chipper voice. Robert came behind me, a big smile on his face.

"Hey guys," Ross said. He anxiously fiddled a pencil, banging it against the desk.

"You're here early," I said.

"I'm waiting for something," was his only reply.

"What?"

"Just something."

"Something? Or someone?"

Ross looked up at me.

"What?"

"I was just wondering. You get Emmitt Smith yet, or is Sam still stalling?"

Ross shot me a wide-eyed look.

"How'd you know about that? Did Sam run his mouth?"

It was Robert's turn now to have some fun.

"Ross," Robert said. "Have you actually been talking to Sam about this? I mean, has he been calling you?"

There was unmistakable confusion on Ross's face. He still hadn't put two and two together.

"No, we've been going back and forth on e-mail. Why?"

"Just curious," Robert said.

Ross sensed the tension in the air. Something was going on, he knew that. What that was, he was completely out of the loop.

"Why did you ask that?" he said after looking at Robert's and my grins. "And how do you know about the trade in the first place?"

I shrugged. Mr. Cool was clearly getting agitated. He stood up from his desk and walked over to us.

"Start talking."

Robert feigned concern.

"You positive those e-mails came from Sam?" he asked Ross.

"Who else would be sending them?"

"I don't know. I mean, you hear the stories about hackers and all."

"With the subject line 'fantasy football trade'?"

Robert stifled a laugh. Ross looked at him, then at me. I couldn't hold it back any longer. The smile on my face was as wide as a river. The cogs in Ross's head started turning. His eyes narrowed as he looked at the both of us. The picture was getting clearer.

"What are you guys up to?" he said finally.

"Why don't you just double check there, Ross. Just to be on the safe side."

"Dammit," Ross said. He went back to his computer and started sifting through his e-mails. Robert and I watched intently as Ross re-read the e-mails in question. Ross stared at the screen for a few moments and then forced the air from his lungs in a long exasperated sigh.

"You guys are jerks!" he barked at us as we clapped with joy. "You were behind this whole thing."

"Hey, don't blame us," I countered. "If you could use e-mail like everyone else in the world, we would never have pulled the wool down over your eyes."

Robert and I high-fived. It was better than I expected. The expression of my brother's face was priceless. He just stared with the blank expression of one who has finally realized he was on the receiving end of a well-planned, well-executed practical joke.

"Okay, okay, you two pulled one over on me... finally," Ross conceded. "But just remember, paybacks are hell."

For the next several days, I waited for Ross's retaliatory strike, yet none came. This didn't concern me at first, but as the days dragged into weeks, and no repercussions surfaced, I was getting more anxious and more worried. Eventually, I was lulled into the security that the fantasy football season had consumed Ross's attention and that he had forgotten all about our prank. As the weeks wore on, I put it behind me as well. Neither Ross nor I won the fantasy football season. My attention went back to work and golf. My game was steadily improving through a combination of private lessons, constant repetition, and finally developing a feel for the game.

Images of joining the senior golf tour played in my head every time I drove three hundred yards from the tee, or made eagle on a par hole.

In early December, I received a Christmas card in the mail from one of our sponsor banks. In the card was a voucher for a free round of golf for four at a posh course in Dallas. The gift couldn't have come at a better time for me, and needless to say, my excitement permeated throughout the office. At that time, the course was considered the best in the Dallas area, and I had wanted to play there since I first took up a club. I asked my brother Martin, Robert, and Dorsey, who were my usual golf partners, if they would join me.

On the way to the golf course that weekend, I handed the voucher to Robert and asked him to put it in his pocket. He held it in his hands a few moments before tucking it into his shirt pocket.

"You'd think with all the money that a bank makes they could afford better graphics," he said.

"It's a voucher. They probably didn't want to waste money on a piece of paper that's ultimately going to be thrown out," I replied

"Good point," he said, "but still."

It was true. The voucher was less than impressive, but a bank makes money for a reason. Investing money into non-money making ventures was not one of them. A voucher doesn't bring in clients; a round of golf at an upscale country club golf course did. End of story.

We parked the car and strode into the golf pro shop. The manager behind the desk was the iconic image of the golf course gatekeeper. He was in his fifties, slightly balding, and wore bilious plaid pants and a white polo shirt with the title "manager" embroidered in blue across his heart. I passed him the voucher and told him we wanted a tee time.

He studied the voucher in his hands a few moments then looked up at us.

"Where did you get this?" he said gruffly.

"It was a gift from a business associate," I explained.

"Some gift," he snorted and tossed the voucher into a waste paper basket.

"What did you do that for?" Martin chimed in.

"This is the finest golf course in Dallas, not a car wash. We don't give out vouchers that look like this."

"With all due respect, sir," I said trying to keep my anger at an even keel, "that was a voucher from one of the finest banks in Dallas. I'm pretty damn sure they are not in the habit of running off counterfeit golf vouchers. Do you think it's possible that it's a new format that you haven't seen redeemed yet?"

"Sir, I've worked here over twenty years. There isn't a piece of paper that's released from here that I haven't seen. You want to pay for a round of golf or not?"

Dorsey and I looked at each other. I couldn't understand what was happening, but was not going to let some misunderstanding prevent me from playing that day.

"Look, here's what I can do. I'll leave you my credit card number and phone number, and if you cannot prove the voucher's authenticity with your supervisor, you can charge my credit card for our play here today. How does that sound?"

"Like a paying customer."

The day was great. There's such a difference playing on a public golf course and a private one. Greens are manicured, divots replaced, sand traps meticulously raked. The place just demands that you play better. We all played fairly well and enjoyed the course.

Returning to the pro shop we discovered that the voucher was in fact not legitimate. Nonplussed, I paid for the round and the four of us went to the parking lot. On the way home, Ross called me on my cell phone.

"How was the course?" he asked cheerfully.

"It was amazing. Best one I have ever been on," I responded enthusiastically.

"Really? You saw the course?"

"I just told you I did. How could I play without stepping foot on it?"

"You actually played it?" Ross sounded stupefied. "Everything went smoothly? No problems?"

"Not exactly. I had to spring for the entire round. Turns out the voucher..." and then I stopped talking. It hit me like a ton of bricks. The voucher was from Ross. He had orchestrated the whole thing. I wondered if the poor graphics on the voucher was his way of sticking it to me for riding him about his lack of computer skills. "Ross, you're a son of a bitch," I said when I heard him start to crack up on the line.

"Consider it payback, boys!" And with that, he hung up the phone.

I turned to Martin and the guys and shook my head.

"Looks like he got us good," I said to him.

"You're kidding," he said. We were all floored.

"I'm out four hundred bucks for today's round. Our fantasy football prank just got costly."

We rode in silence the rest of the way. With what would be a theme running through most of our adult lives, Ross had balanced the scales yet again.

Chapter Nine

At this time, our company marked a true milestone: the sale of our first merchant portfolio, which included all of the companies with whom we had contacts, to a firm named TMP. After the sale of the portfolio, we would receive a substantial one-time payout for our efforts. Ultimately, the transaction paid handsomely, earning Ross and me substantial financial remuneration.

Overall, the deal generated over one million dollars for our company, a figure that five years ago would seem little more than a dream, no less a reality. After the deal had been finalized, and all of the "t's" crossed and the "i's" dotted, the CEO of TMP, Tim Weeks, and his Senior Vice President, Tony Green, flew to Dallas to spend a few days to celebrate the mutually profitable endeavor. Tim was an avid golfer and asked Ross and me to join Tony and him at one of Dallas' most upscale golf courses, a place called Tour 18. While being a course accessible to the public, what made Tour

18 exceptionally unique was that each hole was an exact replica of a famous hole in the U.S. Each hole provided you the opportunity of envisioning yourself on the elite of the elite; bunkers and water hazards mirrored to perfection the complexity of Cherry Hill, Winged Foot, TPC Sawgrass, Pebble Beach, and of course, Augusta. For an impassioned fan of the sport, Tour 18 was akin to playing baseball in Yankee Stadium or racing at the Indy 500.

The four of us played an enjoyable front nine; the company was amicable, the atmosphere congenial, and the weather a shade below perfect. But as typically happens when four men are engaged in some level of athletic competition, the testosterone rises, and egos get in the way of better judgment. As we walked to the tenth tee, Tony asked Ross if we'd like to spice things up and make a friendly wager on the nine remaining holes.

Ever the gambling aficionados, Ross and I were eager to further capitalize on our good fortune in a test of skill. Furthermore, such a contest seemed appropriate on the golf course, as well as a way to solidify a good relationship with TMP. After all, we had just made a lucrative profit because of our association with these guys. A gesture of good faith didn't strike me as an unreasonable request.

That said, we were not looking to lose any of our profit because of over aggressive wagering. Tim was an outstanding golfer – about a one or two handicap at the time. While Ross and I were not slouches on the fairway, Ross was about an eight handicap, and I was at five. Still, our talent was in the initial stages of development where Tim's had been honed by countless more hours at the craft, not to mention the business deals merged traversing over eighteen holes. Factoring in Tony's participation with Tim (up until that point, Tony didn't demonstrate any of the nuances associated with capable golfers; his swing was off, his patience thin, and his capacity to read the breaks on the green, flawed), Ross and I thought we could hold our own and not take too bad a beating.

"How much a hole?" Tony asked.

Ross looked at me. He was jazzed by the betting action, and I could tell he was ready to tear up the back nine. I gave him a shrug.

"Twenty bucks," Ross said.

Tim laughed out loud.

"Twenty," he said. "Twenty is what I tip the valet at the restaurant. I was thinking something a little more interesting."

"What did you have in mind?" I inquired.

"Fifty per man? You can do fifty. You just made a million."

Ross and I again shared another look. Knowing I was the better golfer, he was looking for some sign from me that it was okay to proceed. I nodded my head, and he turned to Tim and stuck out his hand.

"You're on," Ross said.

The men shook. The match was on.

Ross and I easily parred the tenth hole and found ourselves up fifty dollars when Tony missed a ten foot put on the green. The early success was key as it made me feel more comfortable and allowed me to ease in the game for the first time since Tony suggested we play for cash. Ross and I high-fived each other, as Tim playfully grabbed Tony around the neck, messing up his hair.

As Tim teed up his ball on the eleventh hole, he turned to us.

"Let's press it," he said. "What do you say? You're one up; give us a chance to take it back."

I was confused. I turned to Ross who stood there with a similar bewildered expression on his face.

"Press what?" I asked finally.

Tim broke out into a wide grin, and started chuckling. I couldn't help but notice the patronizing tone to his laugh, as if he couldn't believe we hadn't heard the term before.

"Pressing it means doubling the money. Instead of fifty bucks this hole, let's make it a hundred. You know, in the spirit of sportsmanship."

"You wouldn't be even," I countered. "You'd be up fifty bucks."

"What's life if you don't take chances?" he said.

I stood there a few moments. Tim didn't get to where he was in business without being shrewd. I couldn't shake the feeling that we were being taken, but the die had already been cast. Somewhat reluctantly, Ross and I agreed to press the hole, which we ended up losing. Tim grinned at us as he picked out his ball from the cup. It was going to be a long back nine.

The funny thing about adversity is that it can make or break a person depending on how they handle it. While Ross and I were not as skilled as Tim, what we lacked in ability we made up in perseverance. By the time we reached the sixteenth hole, Ross and I found ourselves up $450. Tim and Tony's early success on number eleven had not been repeated. That's the way with luck; it goes one way for a while, but it goes the other way too.

Number sixteen was worth $900 because Tim and Tony pressed the hole, which unsurprisingly, they did on each and every one after ten. I ended up parring the sixteenth, which Tim bogeyed thanks to a chip from the bunker going awry. Tony was facing a twenty-foot putt downhill for par. I have to say, I was feeling pretty good considering Tony had yet to prove himself with any challenging shots that required that little something extra. Ross shook his head as Tony eyed up his shot; he didn't have a snowball's chance in Hell of making it. But true to the fickleness of luck, Tony sank the impossible putt to tie us on that hole. Tony smiled at us in mock belief.

"Go figure," he said, scooping his ball from the hole.

Ross looked at me and bit his lip slightly. I could tell that he, as well as my own misgivings, was wondering how Tony had hit a putt on a green that had not only one, but two breaks. In fact, as I was walking to the seventeenth hole, I remarked to myself how "good" Tony had become since money was laid on the line. I quickly calculated his scores and discovered much to my chagrin that Tony had parred nearly all of the holes in the back nine. I was in utter disbelief; these men, despite their helicopters and designer clothing, were honest-to-God hustlers.

Ross and I still had two holes to add to our lead, and true to form, our last two holes were our best. We were in that moment of absolute concentration, distancing ourselves from the surrounding environment and living in each individual moment. You could have set a bomb off that day, and we wouldn't have noticed a thing. Each movement was an artistic expression; our backswings were as fluid as an ice dancer's, our putts as graceful as a master's brush stroke. Tim and Tony's play was good, but not good enough. And in the end, the two brothers, the two high school educated businessmen, had pulled it out. By my calculations, Ross and I had cleared $450 each.

"Not too shabby for an afternoon's work," Tim said, congratulating my brother and me as he pulled a thick clip of hundred dollar bills from his pants. He counted out nine crisp Benjamin Franklins and balled them into my outstretched palm.

Although I didn't realize it then, that golf match would prove a prescient moment in what was to follow. It didn't matter whether a man was blue collar or the elite of society, everyone was trying to make a buck and get ahead and would do anything, including tricks and deception, to accomplish that very objective.

One of the good things about my brother Ross is that he has always unflinchingly believed in the "work hard play hard" ethic. So, in celebration of the "after sale" deal the company landed, he threw a party at Joseph's. The original plan was to bring a few of the key members involved in support of the sale and have a few beers and shots to commemorate the occasion. However, a "few" friends had soon turned into a full-fledged blast. When the bar finally closed down, Ross invited the hardcore over to the house for an "after hours" party where the rage continued. What started off as a few soon turned into many as people brought other people who brought more liquor. Music thumped menacingly from the stereo speakers. Women gyrated mercilessly in the limited space between the furniture, their short skirts riding up high. To tell the truth, it was quite the scene.

I was supposed to have called Lynn after the meeting, but one thing had led to another. I was officially five hours late when I found a phone and a quiet room away from the wild rumpus to make my call.

"Hey, gorgeous," I said when Lynn picked up on the other end. Her voice sounded groggy from having been woken from sleep.

Upon hearing my voice, she fell silent. I knew I was in big trouble. Deep trouble.

"Lynn?"

"Yeah?" There was an edge to her tone. Her sleep-heavy voice was soon replaced with irritation. She was not happy.

"I know I should have called you earlier, but things kind of dragged on."

There was a long pause.

"Where are you?"

"Home." It was one word, but I think I slurred it.

"Are you drunk?"

"Nooooo…"

"Is that music? Are you having a party?"

"No. Well, yes. We had a big week. We sold our merchant portfolio and made a ton of money." I grimaced as the words tumbled out of my mouth. The "M" word again. "I didn't mean that," I quickly added.

"Yes you did. You're proud of it, Adam. You should be. It's a hell of big accomplishment. You and your money should celebrate."

"Lynn..."

At that moment the bedroom door opened and this young girl who had come in with the latest party-crashers popped her head inside. She was pretty and looked as if she worked at a local down-graded version of Hooters. She was holding a bottle of Bailey's in one hand and Reddi-Whip in the other.

"You want a blow job?" she asked, holding up both hands.

"Get out!" I screamed at her. "Can't you see that I'm on the phone?"

"It's just a blow job..."

"What?" Lynn's voice cackled through the phone.

I ignored her and turned my attention back to Lynn.

"It's not what you think...this girl... she's got booze..."

"You don't know what I think. Sad part is, maybe you never did..."

I knew she slammed the phone down because I had to pull my receiver away. It was like someone fired a gun near my ear.

The party girl was still at the door. She looked at me and offered me the Bailey's. I said nothing, took the bottle, and closed the door.

Hooray for me, I thought, and took a long pull from the bottle.

Money is the American dream. Those who don't have it want it, and those that do have it want more of it. If you don't think so, take a look at the next Forbes 100 and ask yourself: how many of these people do what they do just to fill in a forty-hour workweek? Money is a potent motivator, and a generous reward for those who pursue their aspirations. It is an equalizer, a weapon, a crutch, and a shield. There is no good or bad with money; it simply is.

Shortly after the golf match of the century, Ross and I turned our attention toward the low cost, potentially high payoff world of penny stocks. All of our business contacts at the time raved about the money that could be made on the stock market. While it was no surprise that if a person that owned thousands of shares in high value stocks such as in oil companies or GE was flush, it was financially difficult for a person to just buy thousands of shares in these companies. Money makes money is what the adage says. And no one was going to get rich buying just a handful of these well-established power stocks. The key was to find that one cheap unknown stock before it becomes big and sell it when it's value boomed. All you had to do was purchase the right one and a lot of it. And that's how we became involved in trading penny stocks.

A close friend of mine was a financial analyst at the time and immediately tried to persuade me to steer clear of that very volatile and unpredictable world. When I relayed his message to Ross, my brother scoffed. He had done research into the penny stock market, and true to the salesman my brother was, sold me that my friend's warning, while sincere, was just bogus nonsense. Ross was sure he had found the proverbial pot of gold in low priced stock shares.

Ross and I began purchasing stocks at five cents a share. Ross's extensive research had paid off when our initial investments ballooned into two thousand dollars within three days. We had doubled our money in less than seventy-two hours. The excitement of that first windfall took an immediate hold on Ross; like all things he tried that he was successful at, Ross's eyes burned with intensity and enthusiasm, which he used to refuel and channel his efforts. After the first three rounds of successful low-stake investments, Ross convinced me to make a slightly larger purchase. Somewhat reluctantly, I agreed to put up ten thousand dollars. Ross on the other hand anted thirty thousand dollars into the venture. Three days later, we each had doubled our money again.

"We've got to tell our friends," Ross beamed as he tallied his earnings in our office one afternoon. "This is free money. This is a dream come true."

"It's been good," I said, "but things change. The market is the market."

"Thank God it is," he countered, "because I would have had to rob a bank to earn this kind of money in one afternoon."

He had a point, even if I hated to admit it. So Ross and I began contacting all of our friends, eager to cut them in on the action. We explained to them how we had doubled our income in a few short weeks by playing the penny stock market through shrewd investment choices. After all, it wasn't a sales pitch; this wasn't some half-brained pyramid scam or get rich quick scenario. It was our way of sharing our good fortune with those who knew us when. Many of them were intrigued by the prospect, and without much convincing, got in on the penny stock craze as well. Soon, we were operating our own little network of penny stock traders. Each morning, Ross and I would sit at our computer terminals and stare at the monitors waiting for the day's trading to begin. There was a palpable excitement to this new endeavor, and like anything we put our minds to, we jumped in feet first, immersing ourselves in this new business opportunity. As the days wore on, we became less inclined to leave our computers since the stocks were updated every fifteen minutes. We got so organized that we planned our day in fifteen-minute increments so we'd never be otherwise engaged in other business matters when an update was posted.

On one occasion, Ross had identified what he termed the "next great stock," which was selling for approximately one dollar a share. This was it, is how he phrased it. The big one. The one on which all of our retirement aspirations could rest. He was committing himself, he said. One hundred thousand shares. It was the last ticket we'd ever have to buy to Easy Street.

Being the more cautious of us two, I bought only 25,000 shares. Get rich quick ideas rarely came to fruition, and for every over night success story there was, I'm sure there were a thousand examples of people who went belly-up from poor investment decisions. The majority of our friends followed Ross's lead scooping up as many shares as they could afford to. True to form, Ross's instinct paid off. Within a week, the stock had doubled in value. There was talk about whether to sell now or ride the wave, but everyone deferred to Ross who was certain the stock price would go up one more cycle. After another week, the stock value rose to $2.50 a share. It was time. The group sold our shares with each one of us clearing a sizable profit. While the profit wasn't exactly enough to quite our day jobs, there was plenty of extra cash that made up for my brother's hyperbole.

Our mother had remarried since our move to Dallas. The guy's name was Allen, and for all intent and purpose, he was a decent enough guy that made a steady living, and more importantly, treated our mom the way she deserved to be treated. He too got involved in the penny stock market and was quickly on board with every move that my brother made. The only difference, however, was that Allen was more relaxed, often waiting longer to sell after the rest of us did. And to give the guy his due, sometimes that extra week turned into a bigger return on his investment. So when the rest of us got out, Allen waited. The hold out proved a lucrative decision; the "retirement" penny stock hit its peak at $9.00 a share. Ross was kicking himself for selling too soon. When Allen sold his shares, he had enough money to buy his new boat, a fact that he liked to share with us every time the family got together.

However, Allen's good fortune was a turning point. Luck goes one way, but it goes the other way too, not just on the golf course, but in all facets of life. Allen's payday seemed to drain our penny stock enterprise of its previous successes, and we never again had a significant play as we had before. Every stock Ross picked after Allen's financial bonanza turned into a disappointment; we either broke even or lost money on the transactions. The penny stock venture lasted a few more months before we decided to extricate ourselves from Wall Street. When all was said and done, we still cleared a few thousand dollars, but like any gambler that plays roulette will tell you, you can only stick out so many bad turns of the wheel before you take your chips and move on. While money was made, none of us, including Ross, ever held onto the huge sums of money we made in the beginning. Still, regardless of the outcome, the penny stock episode of our lives was an entertaining diversion from our daily business practices. We had worked long and hard to enjoy the kind of freedom we now had, and penny stock trading gave us the opportunity to not only enjoy the financial success we had attained, but to take chances to increase it through other ventures.

Chapter Ten

Another milestone was reached when Ross and I purchased our first building for the business. We had needed a larger office space for quite some time, and now that our business could accommodate over 100 employees, we took the next step in our careers and secured 15,000 square feet of useable space complete with seven executive offices on the second floor. The parking lot offered six covered spots behind the office. "A&R Bankcard" was emblazoned in bright blue letters at the front of the building. There is a distinct difference between leasing office space and owning it; ask any businessman. The deed, while just a piece of paper, is a legitimizing force that immediately reinforces credibility in the business world.

On the day we moved to our lush new accommodations, we planned a little moving party and asked several of our friends to pitch in and help us make the transition. Mac and I arrived early before anyone else and set up a spread of coffee and donuts to feed the volunteers. One valuable lesson I had learned during my collegiate experience was that if you want people to show up to a function, it was best to provide free food and drink as an incentive. We immediately began to box up the materials and tear down the cubicles that had made the main floor a labyrinth. Gradually our helpers showed up, helping themselves to the free boxes of Krispy Kremes™ and catching each other up on the past weekend's raucous escapades. I thought that once they had their fill they'd notice Mac and me taping up boxes and start to assist in the process. This was not the case; Mac and I had packed up over 250 boxes with no help from our friends.

"Can you believe they are just standing there watching us bust our asses?" Mac complained as he and I rolled the copier to the elevator.

"You get what you pay for, Mac, and their help is for free."

"You should charge them ten bucks for every donut they stuffed down their throats."

"Next time," I said. "Next time."

We were struggling a bit with the copier when one of the freeloaders noticed. He managed to pry his fingers from a croissant long enough to give us a hand with the copier.

"You guys need a hand?" It was tough to understand him as he was still in the process of chewing.

"You sure?" Mac said sarcastically. "There's a couple of glazed still left in the box."

We pushed the copier into the elevator and descended to the first floor. When the doors opened, Mac, Mr. Good Samaritan, and I wheeled the copier into the lobby of the building. I glanced over my shoulder and noticed a thin but heavy dark line leading back into the elevator.

"Hold up, guys," I said. "What's that on the carpet?"

Mac bent down and inspected the marking.

"Damn," he said rubbing his fingers after he touched the mark. "It's ink."

"The toner's leaking," I said. "Great."

"What do you want to bet we tracked that shit all the way from upstairs?"

"Not the kind of bet I want to win," I said.

Mac and I took the elevator back upstairs. Sure enough, Murphy's Law proved correct once again, as it always did. Things will and do go wrong when you least want them to. As we surveyed the damage, which to say was extensive would be vastly understating the situation, one of our friends offered, between bites of donut, to help clean the mess. The self-sacrifice of his statement must have resounded in a frequency only attune to the ears of those who know they are taking advantage of a person, because everyone started speaking up wanting to help. It was almost comical watching ten people on a sugar fit stumble over each other trying to make themselves useful.

I looked over at Mac and winked.

"You know where the mops are," I said to them. "Clean it up."

While they set to work at cleaning the mess, Mac and I took refuge at the back of the building. The Dallas sun was high and bright, and the heat was beginning to bore down on the city in a persistent burn. We sat in the warm afternoon glow, chugging well-deserved beers. Before I had moved out here, if you had told me that I'd get used to the weather in Texas, I would have bet my savings against it. But there is something comforting in the consistency of Texas weather. The sun is always out, the weather is always warm, and the sky is always blue.

Sitting there in silence, I was longing for the arrival of the movers. While I enjoyed my free time away from the daily grind of business operations, I was anxious to get settled in the new office. That was one of the contradictions in my personality; when I was working, I was anxious to get away; when I was away, my mind was on the business. Right then, while the move was figured into "down time," I just wanted the business to be up and running in its new location. The whole moving process was taking longer and required more work than I had initially anticipated. The morning's delinquency on the part of my friends certainly had not helped the cause any.

The new building holds many special memories for me. Not only did our business thrive, but so did our penchant for practical jokes. We were always trying to find the happy balance between working hard and playing hard, making sure that neither one overtook the other. One of the most legendary pranks of Ross's and my illustrious careers took place in this building, something that has come to be known as the "Carl Incident."

Ross's wife had a friend, Carl, who had long wanted to join our company. He was a nice guy, but he didn't have any actual experience in business. While that was okay when we first started, once we became more established, it wasn't viable or prudent to hire inexperienced sales staff. Ross kept putting him off again and again whenever he inquired about possible employment with us. I knew very little about Carl, so I was content to accept Ross's appraisal of his abilities. However, what I did know about him is that he was a true gamer. He was fearless, and loved dares and practical jokes as much as Ross and I. I always thought anyone that had this trait in him was most likely a person I was going to like. It says a lot about a person if they have the ability to laugh at themselves as easily as at someone else.

For many years, Ross and I had been developing a potential dare that was destined to go down in the book of world records for the courageous soul that accepted and completed its objective. The dare was simple: walk the 200 miles from Dallas to Shreveport, Louisiana. The conditions were not as easy: the walker could not accept any rides or sleep indoors. In fact, the walker could only go inside a building long enough to eat a meal. He could carry with him anything he chose, but he could not default on any of the conditions or else the dare was null and void. This was a dare that would test a person's resilience, physical endurance, patience, and will. In short, it was what we termed "the Grandaddy of Dares."

Ross and I were refining the particulars of the dare when Carl came around asking if he could work for us again. It became almost a monthly routine, with Carl beating around the bush before just flat-out asking my brother if he would hire him. Carl was nothing if he wasn't persistent, which gave Ross the idea of making the dare scenario a reality. Rather than turning Carl down this time, Ross made a proposition: if Carl accepted and completed the dare, the payoff would be $5,000 and a position on the sales team.

"Who in their right mind would agree to this?" I asked Ross later at my apartment when he came over and told me Carl had agreed to the dare.

"I know, but at least this might scare him and get him off my back about the job. I'm running out of excuses."

"What if he gets hurt?"

"He'll quit before he gets hurt."

"I don't know, Ross. It was fun to think about it, but there are so many unknowns that might happen."

"He'll probably back out before he even gets started."

A few weeks passed, and I honestly forgot about the dare. However, one afternoon, Carl showed up at our office in his walking shoes and a well-stocked backpack. He looked like he was about to go on a safari.

"I'm here to start the walk, guys," he explained after Ross asked him if he was going to a costume party.

"The walk?" I asked.

"The dare. You laid down the challenge; I'm picking it up."

Ross and I sat in a stunned silence. While we had long hoped that someone would do the dare, we never figured that anyone would actually do it. People were always talking big; few actually had the guts to back up a bark with a bite. So when Carl had initially agreed to do it, no one expected him to actually follow through. And now here he was dressed to the nines to back up what he had promised.

"Well, a deal's a deal," Ross aid. "You sure you want to go through with this?"

"I'm here, aren't I?" Carl responded, breaking into a smile that would have made the Grand Canyon look small.

So it started. Ross gave Carl his cell phone, instructing him to call daily and report his whereabouts. Carl took the phone, put his headphones on, slung his enormous backpack over his shoulder, and made his way to the front door. As he walked, a crowd had gathered and followed him out the door like he was a rock star. Sporadic applause and shouts of encouragement accompanied Carl who turned around and waved at the office one more time before exiting. Outside, Carl walked down the road. Ross and I stood next to each other as Carl's figure gradually became a dot in the distance.

When Carl was out of sight, I turned to Ross.

"What do you think?" I asked. "He going to do it?"

"No chance. He'll cheat before he does it proper," Ross said.

"Well, I damn sure would. That's a long way to walk without any shelter or rest. I don't think he would have taken the dare if he didn't have some way to get through it without cutting some corners."

Ross frowned. "That's a good point. Tell you what. Let's give him a day or two, and if he doesn't break, we'll know he's cheating."

"How are we going to know that? I'm not following him."

Ross patted me on the shoulder. "Relax, big brother. That's what private investigators are for."

Ross acquired the services of a local P.I. who was a former Dallas detective that had retired from the force and used his talents in less life-threatening endeavors. The first day, Carl was still in Dallas, but he felt good. The second day, however, the tribulations of walking twelve hours a day had begun to set in. Carl contacted us at our pre-scheduled time and sounded exhausted after walking God knows how many miles.

"I'm going to do this," he said finally, after exhaling a long breath. "Don't worry about me."

"Just say the word, Carl, and we'll have someone pick you up. Where are you?"

"Just outside of Dallas, but I'm getting there."

"You sure? No need to kill yourself, man."

"I'm not giving up. It's just a bit harder than I thought. I mean, it's just walking, but my dogs are barking."

When Ross hung up the phone, he smiled.

"What did I tell you? He'll be down and out within forty-eight hours."

The office teemed with a palpable excitement about Carl. Everyone was making wagers and side wagers on whether he was going to give up and when. There wasn't an hour that went by when two people weren't discussing his chances, backing up their assessments with a bet or two.

"Twenty bucks says he'll throw in the towel tomorrow."

"You're on!"

"No way, he'll last till Friday minimum."

"I'll take that bet."

Ross and I walked around the office doing our best imitations of Carl, contorting our bodies as if we were caving under the weight of our backpacks and walking as though our legs were ready to buckle with the next step. There was little doubt that Carl would not complete the dare. He had little going in his favor. First, he wasn't the slightest bit athletic, and even though walking isn't an athlete's sport, Carl had never shown to have any stamina whatsoever. Second, and most important, Carl was a man that liked food – real food – and there were places on the highway where the best he was going to find to eat was vending machine cuisine. So it wasn't like he stood any real chance. People were people, and Carl was, well, Carl.

The third day brought inclement weather to Texas. A series of severe thundershowers were pelting the region, and poor old Carl was stuck out in the rain with only the shelter of his pup tent to shield himself from the rain at night. I'm not going to lie here; I was a bit concerned over Carl's safety. A joke is a joke, but factors threatening your health are another matter entirely. When the time of his phone call arrived, I sat anxiously nearby the phone to hear if he had made it through the night without injury or the comfortable sanctuary of a plush hotel. At the very least, if he called it quits, I wanted to be able to get a car to him and fast.

"It stormed like a beast last night," I told Ross as we waited in our office. "You think he's okay?"

"He's fine. I'm just wondering if the storm forced him into a hotel, and he won't tell us about it. The P.I. isn't on the case yet."

"I wouldn't blame him if he did. I sure would."

"He probably enjoyed a nice hot shower this morning and silver dollar pancakes."

"Better than being dead in the gutter," I said.

When the phone finally rang, I almost accidentally hung up on Carl, I had grabbed the phone so quickly.

"Hey, man," I said into the receiver. "You alright?"

"Put him on speaker," Ross said. I complied. "You still alive?" Ross said.

"Barely. Some storms, eh?" Carl said. He sounded pretty upbeat for a man who survived a Biblical flood.

"How'd you make out last night?" Ross asked.

"Well, it was pretty interesting. I put up my tent in this field off the road. I was pretty safe from the storm, but when I woke up this morning, I felt like someone was watching me."

"Watching you?" I asked. "What do you mean?"

"That's the thing. I figured I was getting paranoid, but when I looked up, I had two cows poking their heads in my tent! Hell of a way to wake up. Took me twenty minutes to shoo them away so I could get my tent packed up."

So Carl hadn't taken refuge indoors. After the phone call, I looked at Ross.

"What do you think?"

Ross was still chuckling over the story.

"Carl isn't funny enough to make up something like that."

"So he slept in the field with the cows?"

Ross nodded. "The man's got guts."

The next day Carl's phone call revealed another odd detail. According to Carl, he was becoming something of a local celebrity throughout the rural towns he was visiting. When he ate in a diner, he chatted up the locals and explained to them about his journey. His story was spreading through word of mouth, and soon diners along his projected path were expecting him. No lie, crowds were gathering to cheer on this evolving folk hero. He was becoming a minor league Forrest Gump.

"All the farmers offer me rides in their pickups," Carl told us on the phone. "But don't worry, I explain I can't take a ride or else I'll lose."

I was dumbfounded. Only in America, I thought. But while I was being won over by Carl's stories, Ross's skepticism was getting the best of him. He had let the cow story slide, but he was not about to believe that a tired man with wobbly muscles and blistered feet was declining rides from his adoring public. Ross contacted the P.I. and told him to check out Carl's "tall tales."

The P.I. followed Carl for two full days. He reported that Carl had discarded his backpack and was now pushing a shopping cart along the road. When Ross and I heard that, we were quite impressed with his creativity. Here was this guy, stripped of all comfort and safety, pushing a shopping cart like a bag lady just to win a job that we would have given him (eventually) without all of this drama. Carl had a stronger constitution than we had seen at first glance.

But Ross wasn't completely sold that Carl had gotten this far without accepting a gift from the kindness of strangers. He asked the P.I. to see if Carl would accept a ride. When the P.I. called to report Carl's reaction, Ross was certain that he would hear that Carl accepted the P.I.'s offer.

Ross's smile slowly dissipated from his face as he listened to the P.I.

"Okay, thanks."

"Well?" I said after Ross hung up the phone.

"Go figure. He didn't accept it. The P.I. tried a couple of approaches but Carl didn't bite. He said he was on a dare. He didn't cheat."

The investigator's report brought Ross around. This guy really wanted to be part of our company. And heck, why not? He deserved it. Lord knows I wouldn't walk two hundred miles.

By this time, Carl's eleven day trek across two states was nearing its end. Ross decided to rent a bus and take a huge crowd of people to meet Carl when he rolled into Shreveport. We went all out, decorating the bus with signs and had champagne on hand to toast Carl's odyssey. As we mingled around the bus, we saw the walking man coming toward us in the distance with shopping cart in tow. When he got closer, the group started cheering and clapping. Carl's face broke into a huge grin. He loved every minute of it, despite the fact that he looked like a road vagabond. He was covered in dust and dirt from head to toe, smelled like something that had died three days before, and had eleven days worth of stubble poking out of his chin. But still, here he was, no worse for wear. And true to our word, on the next Monday, Carl had a desk and a nameplate on the sales force floor. Carl turned out to be a solid employee, and he stayed with us for about two years.

Chapter Eleven

The press we got from the sale of the portfolio gave us credibility. Our phone lines lit up like Christmas trees from new clients, and if I thought the green was coming in back then, it was nothing like it was doing now. Someone once said, "When it rains, it pours," but this was of typhoon proportions. Ross was at the top of his game. He was so hot he could sell ice to the Eskimos and ask them to pay double what they wanted to pay.

Still, while work continued its seemingly endless upward trend, things with Lynn had stalled something fierce. After the "blow job" incident, she refused to see me or take my calls. I even went with "old reliable" – two dozen long-stemmed white roses and a card full of self-flagellating mea culpa, but to no avail. When I went by her place an hour after the deliveryman made his round, much to my chagrin I found the remains of the roses in the garbage can out front. The writing was on the wall. I had hit an impasse, and worse, for something that I didn't even do. Yes, there were girls at the house, and yes, the misunderstanding was very "Three's Company"-like, but I didn't touch, kiss, or fool around with *any* other woman. More importantly, I didn't want to. One moment, my brother and I had made the biggest move of our careers, and the next, it was like Mick Jagger and the band had suddenly come over to the house for an impromptu celebration. I couldn't explain it; it just happened. The only thing I did know was that my fidelity and integrity remained intact. My friends tried to convince me to get past her and move on. Women were like busses, they said. Another was bound to come by sooner or later. There were more lame comparisons from guys who dated with the inconsistency and longevity of a carnival ride.

One night, Ross and I were discussing a potential business venture with a big time company in New York that had expressed interest in purchasing A&R Bankcard. We sat at the kitchen table, papers strewn in front of us. Ross was talking, but to be honest, my head wasn't in the conversation, and it showed on my face. Ross was pointing out something to me on a piece of paper. When he looked up at me and saw me zoning, he slapped his hand down on the table.

"You want to listen to this? It kind of affects you too."

"I know. I'm sorry."

"Sorry doesn't pay the rent. Adam, this is a –"

"Big deal," I interrupted. "When isn't it?"

Ross was about to say something but thought better about it. Instead, he took a couple of deep breaths, drumming his fingers on the table.

"Lynn?" he asked me finally.

"I haven't eaten in two days. I'm working on no sleep. What do you think?"

"I think you need to talk to her, is what I think."

"Tough to talk to someone who doesn't answer your calls."

"You tried the flowers?"

"She cut the heads off the stems."

"Ouch," Ross said. "She's pissed, bro."

"You think?" I said sarcastically.

"So go see her." My brother, the pragmatist.

"You think I haven't thought of that? With my luck, she's taken out a restraining order on me."

"Look, Adam. At the risk of sounding like a broken record, this is kind of a big deal. I need your head in the game, which means you need to get whatever it is messing you up set straight. Work it out one way or another. We land this deal, we're set for life. Our families are set for life. This is what we've dreamed about since we were kids sharing a bedroom. We're not going to screw this up."

I looked at Ross. He sat back and took a pull from his beer bottle. The thing about my brother was that he had always had the capability to reduce a problem to its base. In his eyes, there was always a simple solution to a problem, no matter how seemingly complex it was.

"Take care of business, bro," he said.

I smiled at him.

"Okay, Elvis," I replied.

"So leave the damn building already."

The next day I parked myself out in front of Lynn's apartment building. I was motivated. I had coffee, bagels, sunflower seeds, soda – everything needed for a lengthy stakeout. As I waited for her, I rehearsed what I was going to say, pacing back and forth in front of my car. I got more than my share of odd looks from people walking down the sidewalk, occasionally glancing over their shoulders at me as they passed by, wondering if I was a deranged person or just one of the hopeless. At this juncture, I was probably somewhere in between.

By three p.m., I had exhausted my stakeout supplies and needed to go to the bathroom for the third time. Just as I was going to head into a convenience store (the cashier had informed me on my previous visit that I would have to buy a pack of gum to use the restroom), I saw Lynn walking down the street juggling a couple of grocery bags in her arms. As she approached, she nearly dropped them when she saw me waiting for her out front. I tried a big smile to put her at ease; it had the opposite effect, if any.

"Can we talk?" I asked.

She didn't say anything for a few moments and then started to walk to her apartment. My heart sank. It was over. As I removed the car keys from my pocket, Lynn piped up.

"You coming or not?"

Inside her apartment, Lynn poured us two sodas and handed me a glass. She sat down next to me on her sofa but kept a guarded distance, careful not to have her leg brush up against mine.

"So it's about work again."

"If this goes through, I'm set, Lynn." I looked into her eyes and saw the disappointment. I quickly corrected myself. "We're set."

"It's always going to be something, Adam."

"Not this time. I promise. This means no more work. No more meetings or client dinners or office moves. This is the brass ring. A non-stop vacation. Wherever you want to go."

"Where do *you* want to go?" She didn't attempt to hide her tonal inflection.

"Anywhere you want."

"That's not what I mean. You said so yourself. You've been working toward this moment all your life. Well, now it's at your doorstep. Where do you see yourself? What are you going to do then?"

She made a good point. To be honest, I hadn't thought that far ahead. People always talk about what they'd do if they won the multi-million dollar lottery. But traveling the world is not a three hundred and sixty-five-day-a-year occupation. Eventually, it's going to get old if you don't have a plan.

"Ever since I was a kid, Lynn, I dreamed of being rich. When I quit school, I started working because I knew it was going to take a lot of sweat and backache to make something of myself. I wasn't afraid of it; I was willing to do what it took and then some. And now it's all paid off. But to be painfully honest, I never considered the next step until talking with you. I realize now, more than ever, that success really means nothing."

"And why is that?"

"Because success is only worthwhile if you can share it with a person you love."

It took a couple of moments before the magnitude of what I had said sank into her. When it did, Lynn almost did a double-take.

"You love me?" she asked when she was able to formulate the words.

"Yeah. Yeah I do." I smiled. At first I wasn't sure if Lynn was going to kiss me or hit me. She threw her arms around my neck and nearly snapped three vertebrae pulling me close to her.

"I love you too, Adam. But I'm scared. I'm scared that you'll get bored and slip back into the rat race."

"Not me," I promised. "I will never get back into the rat race. I like cats too much."

Lynn smirked and slapped me playfully, a gesture that I had come to appreciate as our little sign of affection. The tumultuous waters had finally stilled. We were back in good standing.

Meanwhile, the business was going well. We did our thing, and we were pretty successful. Clients were coming in and we were all making plenty of money. The thing about a business is if you're into what you're doing, you never really know how successful you are. Sure, income is always a basic barometer, but if you don't pay close attention, you don't have an idea of your company's impact in your respective field. You just love what you do, and you get paid well for doing it. That's one way of judging success.

Still, there is another way. Ross and I discovered how well we were doing when we were approached by BGL, a large associate of ours, about a potential buyout. Now, this was a big deal because BGL was a solid, profitable, and respected business, a New York-based investment firm specializing in purchasing companies in our industry. The fact that this entity wanted to buy us out said not only that we were making the right moves, but also that we were getting so good that a bigger company wanted us. Our company's value had hit an all time high, and honestly, the proposed deal couldn't have come at a better time, as Ross's and my relationship had hit some rough spots. It was the first time we had hit a trying time, and we were contemplating going our separate ways in order to preserve our family ties.

As you can imagine, there is only one real thing that can cause brothers to fight: a woman. But in this case, it's not what you think. It all started when Ross approached me about hiring Lisa Prattle, a high-profile risk management specialist with twenty year's experience being a hired gun. If it was broken, she could fix it. Your company needed some fat trimmed off? Well, she just had the shears for the job. She was methodical and calculating, much the way I envisioned a shark was. If there was blood in the water, God help you.

Once we bought the new building, Ross and I had set a goal to make our business the number one producer among our sponsor bank's clients; currently, we were the second most successful producer, and although this ranking was indicative of a solid business model and unequaled sales track, we both smarted over our silver medal position. Ross believed that Lisa had the killer instinct that we needed to vault ourselves into the pole position.

Basically, I was skeptical about creating a position for Lisa. First and foremost, I have never been an advocate of paying someone – anyone – an exorbitant salary in order to save money. I don't need an MBA from Wharton to see that it doesn't make fiscal sense. Furthermore, I felt slighted by Ross's commitment to Lisa. Risk management had been one of my areas of responsibility, and I felt that I had been doing a damn good job, especially since I earned my stripes on a day-to-day basis. Who was this woman who knew nothing about our company to come in here and start pissing to mark her turf? Despite my severest opposition to the new addition, Ross hired her anyway.

Suffice to say, almost immediately our profits took a hit. Big surprise. It seems Lisa's touch was more brass than golden. Under her helm, we were hemorrhaging money. Her first three "recommendations" were disasters. This wouldn't have been so bad if her fourth suggestion, which involved personnel consolidation, didn't turn out to be a big mistake. There is a general rule that most businesses adhere to: if it's not broken, don't fix it. Our sales staff was our bread and butter, and even in our most lean times, they were the ones that brought in customers. Once the consolidation experiment flopped on its face, even Ross knew that Lisa and the company had to part ways. In the end, although Lisa's tenure with us was much shorter than anyone had anticipated, it was long enough to make a financial dent in our once nearly impregnable veneer.

To compensate for the Lisa fiasco, Ross tightened the company's purse strings considerably. My colleague and friend Robert (who helped me in managing the day-to-day operations) and I soon found ourselves on the proverbial shit-end-of-the-stick. As if our normal twelve-hour work days weren't bad enough, we were soon working fourteen-hour days. First, I had to suffer the indignity of letting an outsider tell us what to do, but now I had to work harder than I already was to make up for Ross's poor hiring decision. Each time Robert and I were burning the midnight oil, Ross left the office at his usual time. When I asked him where he was going, he would just say an important meeting. He wasn't even a good enough liar to make up a more compelling story. Suffice it to say, I was feeling twelve levels below underappreciated, and part of me thought that Ross intentionally was working me like the shrewd businessman he was, expecting his brother to shoulder the burden of weathering Lisa's incompetence until the company righted itself.

I was stunned. I always knew my brother knew his stuff and that his drive for success was nearly unmatchable, but that was the first moment I saw my brother in the leagues of a Donald Trump, with savvy to match his smarts. That night Ross and I discussed the BGL pitch for hours, trying to look at it from all angles to maximize our profit margin. In the end, there were two decisions on the table: one, to take the offer, which still involved a great deal of money, and two, see how genuine the BGL intent was to buy our company, and if that seriousness translated into a more lucrative offer. The president of BGL, Frank Daniels, flew down from New York for a week, along with an extensive research team who perused all of our business records. They made quite the impression in the office, usurping one of the conference rooms and filling it with stacks of files. Number crunchers always look the same, and none that I have ever met has done anything to dispel the myth or image of a geek. They can be great guys, but they still look like they enjoy plaid shirts, bow ties, and glasses that are always too big for their faces.

At the close of the week, we took Frank out to dinner at one of the better restaurants in Dallas. We had barely finished our drinks when Frank wrote a number on a cocktail napkin and passed it over to us. It was larger than the first offer, but wasn't in the neighborhood we were expecting.

"Well, boys?" Frank said, sipping his single malt. "We got ourselves a deal?"

One look at Ross and I knew he was feeling what I was feeling. And this being his bailiwick, I sat in silence and let my brother do what he did best.

"It's a nice offer, Frank," Ross said. "But I'd be lying to tell you that this is what we were looking for, and if our mom taught us anything, it was not to lie."

Frank sat back in his seat. I could see his eyes searching my brother's face for a tell. He was very much like a professional poker player, looking for some sign, some chink in the armor, before he made his play. After what seemed like ten minutes, but was actually probably more about two, Frank leaned on the table.

"What figure did you have in mind?" he asked Ross.

Ross took out a Mont Blanc and scratched a number onto the cocktail napkin. I saw the figure and did my best not to cough up the drink I just swallowed.

Frank looked at that figure. His face showed no emotion. God, I thought to myself, this is how multi-billion dollar business mergers must go, with both sides not trying to give an inch and lose a few million.

"That's a bit high," he said finally.

"Yours was a bit low," Ross countered.

"You boys are smart. I like that. You made something out of nothing and did it well enough to be in the situation you're in right now. But there are things that need work."

"Like what?" Ross asked.

"Your record keeping is not what it could be. There's a lot of grey area. Grey is a color tax people don't like. They see grey, and they're antennae go up. Now, it would be a poor move on my part to acquire something that isn't quite right. A very poor move. You understand?"

After dinner, Ross and I decided that we needed to get our bookkeeping in order. Ross had a friend named Blain Douglas who had worked as the assistant to the corporate financial officer of a huge Dallas company. Ross likened him to the Greek mythological hero Hercules, who had cleaned the Aegean stables as one of his impossible labors. Well, Blain did the same type of cleaning only with financial records. Fortunately, Blain was between jobs at the time, so Ross asked him to join us and help get our records into pristine order. As Blain reviewed our latest statements, he was impressed by our enormous growth over a relatively short time span, and he readily agreed to work with us. He was certain he could organize our records and create an accurate sales projection for the future.

Since I worked with our previous bookkeeper, the onus of orientating Blain fell squarely on my shoulders. As we sat there together that first day, I instantly felt good about hiring him. He was well versed in his profession, that much was certain. But what I liked about him is how he didn't lord his vast knowledge over my head. He maintained a professional, courteous manner about him, and what's more, he seemed eager to sink his teeth into the task at hand. He reminded me of the guys we had first hired, full of piss and vinegar and ready to take on the world. Over the course of the following weeks, Blain proved to be in fact cut in the mold of Hercules; not only was he a fine accountant, he had developed a system to implement within the company to improve our ability to track our profits. This is how legends were made; they not only get the job done, but they also find innovative practices to improve the way the job is done in the future.

As weeks stretched into months, the business continued to grow, and by grow, I mean grow big. A good baseline rule of thumb to ascertain how big your company is getting is by the number of gainfully employed staff buzz around the floor in a beehive of activity. When Blain first started, he was the sole purveyor of all financial matters. Now, he had two people under him and was lobbying hard for an additional two bodies to keep pace with the company's growth. Ross and I had known for quite some time that at this pace our current office space would be insufficient, and we needed to acquire a larger facility to keep pace with our expansion. Fortunately for us, a piece of prime real estate was available just two miles from our current location. This land could easily accommodate a building with over 30,000 square feet, and there was room for a smaller building to be added when the time came to expand once more. There was little deliberation; we purchased the land.

Almost twelve months to the day, we heard again from Frank, the BGL president. His company was again interested in talking to us about a buy-out. He had kept a close watch over the company seeing how we had been managing ourselves. It was time to talk turkey, he said, only this time in New York.

Lynn kept me company as I packed my suitcase for the trip. My hands were shaking a bit as I haphazardly tossed underwear, socks, and a business suit into the black bag. Prior to our departure date, Ross sat me down and told me of his plan: regardless of what was on the table, he was going to make a counteroffer. I wasn't thrilled with the idea, but Ross was persuasive. In all fairness, his decisions had been pretty spot-on since I followed him into the business. Lynn wasn't too happy when I told her the plan. In retrospect, I can't say I blamed her too much. It seemed that, despite everything I had told her, the exact opposite happened.

"Is that smart?" she asked. "Countering like that? What if they walk away?"

"He thinks they won't. They waited a year. They want us bad."

"I'm not asking what he thinks, Adam. I'm asking what you think."

"I think I'd still be working at Andy's Subs if it weren't for my brother. Everything we've done, everything we've achieved, has been by his guidance."

"Have you decided what you want to do after this is all over?"

"Open a little café. Serve drinks, some good food. Have a nice comfortable atmosphere."

"Now that sounds like a plan, Stan."

"I may need some art for the walls, you know."

"I know a good artist. She's expensive though," Lynn teased.

"She have a resume?"

"She's the best."

I took her in my arms and squeezed.

"It's almost over, babe."

"You keep telling me that, but somehow it never quite is."

"I know. I'm sorry."

"Make it up to me then."

"What do you want?"

"A café that houses my ridiculously good paintings on its walls."

I kissed her. Her mouth melted me, and the more I kissed her, the deeper I got lost in its warmth.

That afternoon, Ross, Blain, and I were sitting in first class on a trip to the Big Apple. On the plane, the three of us mulled over just what the offer would entail and for how much money.

"It'll be higher," Ross said, sipping his soda and glancing out the window.

"It has to be," Blain offered. "Your finances are in order, and you only got bigger. We're talking some serious *dinero*."

"How serious?" I asked. "Serious, or Christopher Walken in *Pulp Fiction* serious?"

Ross and Blain looked at each other. They had the same thought and practically said it at the same time.

"Chris Walken serious!"

I ripped up a barf bag and handed a piece to Blain and Ross.

"Write down what you think the bid will be. Closest person gets fifty bucks," I said.

As I sat there hypothesizing what the amount might entail, I couldn't help but think back to the moment Ross first approached me with the cell phone idea. How far we had come! All of the long hours, the hustling, the hirings, and firings had all led to this moment: thirty thousand feet in the sky, drinking champagne, and trying to determine not if we're going to live on Easy Street, but just exactly what houses on that street were we going to buy.

New York City has the reputation of being the best city in the world, and you would be hard pressed to find someone who hasn't been there at least once in their life. They may like it or hate it, but there is always an opinion about the place. Its unequalled skyline, the "city that never sleeps" lifestyle, and truly the best pizza around are reasons indicative of that monument and testament of success on the island of Manhattan. I have always enjoyed coming to New York; while I know that I could never live there, it still remains one of my favorite places to go and spend a weekend.

When we arrived in New York, a limousine met us at the airport and whisked us directly to BGL's headquarters downtown. If you have never ridden in a limousine in New York City, I strongly recommend renting one once and experiencing the city from a different perspective. Trust me. It will be difficult to wipe the smile from your face as you watch the city unfold around you, observing the hustle and bustle of people who are out there to get things done, people driven by their own consciousness, fears, ambitions, and a desire to leave a mark on the city's impervious armor.

BGL's offices were impressive and made ours look humble. Everything was expansive; spacious hardwood floors, everything gleaming and polished, the glass smudge-free. We endured a long presentation in the conference room, drowned in an endless supply of power point and pie graphs. Once the presentation concluded, there was a long question-and-answer period where the three of us were bombarded with probing inquiries about all facets of our operation. Depending on what was asked, Ross, Blain, or I parried their thrusts with aplomb. I couldn't help but think this was some kind of test to see if we were just lucky kids, or businessmen to be reckoned with.

That evening, Frank took us out to a much needed dinner in an intimate bistro with soft lighting and a hell of a veal chop. Over cognacs and brandy, Frank made his pitch. The offer was substantially higher than a year previously. All of our hard work to rectify the problematic areas of the company had paid off – literally. The offer was nearly ten times what it had been just twelve short months earlier.

"Take a day to think it over," Frank explained. "Enjoy the city. Get a Nathan's dog. See a show."

After Frank left, the three of us sat there stupefied. Ross was the first one to shake free from the moment. He signaled over the waiter and ordered all of us a round of vodka on the rocks.

"It's toast time!" he said, beaming.

The waiter returned and set a generous drink in front of each of us. Even Blain, a lifelong teetotaler, understood the magnitude of the moment and hoisted his glass with Ross and me. The glasses made a clear sound as they clinked together. I'll never forget what that drink tasted like; it was to be forever etched into my mind because its taste would be inextricably linked to the moment I had realized my dream.

The next day, the three of us spent a terrific day at Belmont, betting the ponies, laughing, and having a great time. Ross, who had won the closest bid bet, bet his fifty dollars on a long shot in the first race. I immediately understood the significance of the bet; who would have bet on two kids who didn't graduate college to climb their way to the peak of their profession? Ross didn't end up winning, but I liked the fact that he laid money on a dark horse.

As my brother and I played the horses, I thought about our childhood days back in New Jersey, when we used to pretend we were Michael Jordan on the basketball court. Whoever had the ball did their best impersonation of the Great One, driving hard to the basket with our tongues out and wagging, or pulling back in a deft fade-away shot, trying to effortlessly bank the ball off the backboard. Back then, I never would have believed we'd move to Dallas, start our own business, and become millionaires. That was always a dream, tucked safely away in the hours between ten p.m. and six a.m. when anything and everything was possible. And yet there we were, about to close an offer that would financially secure us and our family for life. It was an amazing feeling, and we lived that afternoon in the sanctity of knowing we had achieved what we had set out to do. We started something out of nothing through hard work and ambition and would be rewarded for it by retiring before the age of 40.

When the time came, we piled into our limo and headed back to meet Frank. The world was truly ours.

Chapter Twelve

When you turned the page, I'm sure you thought you'd be reading about how Ross and I would spend our millions, enjoying the fruits of our labor in retirement.

But someone once said something about the best-laid plans of mice and men, and while I still don't exactly understand the meaning of that assertion, I certainly now have an appreciation of what that author was saying.

Bottom line: Ross had decided to hold out.

I'm not kidding.

The night before we went to the track, Ross woke me up and indicated that we needed to talk. He and I crept across the suite so as not to awaken Blain and tip-toed out onto the patio.

"I've been thinking about Frank's offer since we got back from the restaurant," he said.

"I know. It's hard to sleep. That's a lot of money. I've been thinking about what I'm going to do with it," I replied.

"Here's the thing. If Frank thinks our company is worth this much now after a year, just imagine the value of it in another three years! We could triple the amount we'll make from the sale."

"What are you saying?" I asked. I knew what he was saying, but perhaps thought that I had missed something.

"We hold out."

"Ross, a bird in the hand…"

"I know what you're thinking. Hear me out. We hold out, our value increases exponentially. We sell then, we could make enough to buy a sports franchise. Think about it. You and me in the owner's box. Swanky parties. Imagine what we could accomplish if we combined all we know about running a business with our genuine love of sports."

I didn't say anything at first. I wasn't surprised that my brother was having second thoughts. He was always thinking two moves ahead, figuring out the angles to maximize potential profits. And honestly, we had gotten this far on his instinct for making such moves. Still, it was a lot to lose if something happened, and there was a lot of money on the table already.

"A sports franchise. Now that would be something," he said.

Ross and I had long talked about owning a sports team. When we used to share a bedroom in New Jersey, we'd lie awake at night and discuss the trades we'd make and the players we'd draft. At that time, we'd always wanted to buy the Yankees; what kid in New Jersey didn't? But it was all a harmless pipedream; now, it seemed a tangible reality.

I looked at Ross. His face shone with the same excitement when he first told me about the cell phone business.

"What do you think?" he said.

"I think you'd give Steinbrenner a run for his money."

"So it's decided."

"I'm with you. Good or bad, we're brothers. You got us this far, take us the rest of the way."

Ross grinned and punched my arm playfully.

"Frank will be pissed," I said.

"It's business."

"When should we tell him?"

"We go to the track tomorrow like we planned. We enjoy ourselves. We earned it. We got the day to think about it like he said. When we finish up at the track, we let him know our decision."

Frank was not pleased. To his credit, he didn't bitch or moan or get angry. He simply made his best pitch on why we should sell, and when we didn't acquiesce, he stood up, shook our hands, and exited the room. Frank was the consummate professional. He didn't buy our company that day, but he would buy someone else's tomorrow. That's just the way these things work.

When we returned from our New York trip, Ross and I were rejuvenated. Blain had agreed with our decision to hold onto the company.

"You guys are too young to retire. If you didn't have anything to do, you'd go crazy," he said.

He was right. Retiring before 40 seemed like a good idea, until you tried to find out what you were going to do with all of that down-time. And the thing was, retirement was for people who wanted out of the race. But if you still had that fire to compete, the will to do something, accomplish something, then retirement was like putting a thoroughbred in the peek of his career out to stud. The drive was still in us; we owed it to harness it into our new goal of owning a franchise.

Our first order of business was to build a new facility to house the company. After we purchased that prime piece of real estate, we hired contractors and broke ground almost immediately. Ross and I would visit the site and marvel at the structure as it started to go up. It's always fascinating to watch a building go up, to see how the space is transformed by its very essence, and if the architect is good, you can see how the building becomes a natural extension of the very land that it stands upon. If you have ever read *The Fountainhead* by Ayn Rand, you know what I'm talking about. A building should reflect the integrity of the men it's being built for.

In January 2001, we moved into our new offices. In a word, they were outstanding. The executive offices were spacious and plush, more akin to the ones at BGL then our previous office space. The work stations less resembled a bull pen than individual areas of work; roomy and comfortable, they created a favorable environment. The break area was complete with soft leather couches and a big screen television. We were even able to unload our old office building within a few months after opening the new one, which alleviated the expense of dual monthly fees around our necks.

However, not everything goes your way. That's a rule of life, and despite the positive energy of the new vision and new office building, Ross and I were struggling with our team of telemarketers. At first, we had envisioned a large centralized telemarketing center where all of our telemarketers could convene and work. At the time, we had four or five satellite stations throughout the Dallas area with about twenty telemarketers working at each site. While this was convenient for the workers, this was not financially advantageous for us because we had to pay rent for each location, as well as the salary of the managers who oversaw them. Ross refused, and I agreed, that this system was the best one for the company. It was his idea to locate the telemarketing center in prime populous area. That way we'd have no trouble supplementing the telemarketing staff should we lose some of our employees with this move. Eventually, we stumbled upon a vast office space in a well populated area of Dallas that was only a ten minute drive from our new headquarters. We rented the space and relocated our telemarketing enterprise.

To say that all of us were reinvigorated at this time would be a tremendous understatement. There was a palpable excitement in the air that comes from the start of something new, even if it was just an office. The reorganization of the telemarketers coupled with the luxuriousness of the new building helped to create a general sense of happiness. Ross and I purchased an executive suite at the American Airlines Center and often would dole out tickets to sporting events and concerts in order to strengthen and solidify camaraderie among the staff. Employees that had exemplified conduct above and beyond standard practice were rewarded with exclusive seats from which they uld take friends and family to watch the Dallas Mavericks or Dallas Stars. Typically our employees would never have gotten a chance to attend these games, and if they did, not from the prime location of a suite. Ross and I felt good about being able to do this for our employees, some of which had been with us for a long time. We also started throwing casino parties at the end of every year as a holiday/New Year's party. We would rent a large banquet room at an upscale, five-star hotel and hire a casino party company to set up blackjack tables, craps, roulette, and even a few slot machines. A large buffet adorned the back wall and people were free to eat and play as they desired. One thing Ross and I had decided long ago was to share our success, not only with our friends, but also the very people who were instrumental in attaining that success through their perseverance and hard work. Standing there at casino night, watching the high spirits and hearing the laughter of everyone participating seemed to encapsulate how a company should do business: work hard, but play equally hard, and if there was extra in the till, spread out bonuses as deserved.

I took Lynn out to dinner. Things were going well, and I wanted to do something special for her. Once again I was feeling on top of the world – a good business and a good woman. What more did I need?

Walking down the street, we stopped at an ATM so I could withdraw some money. I inserted the card and punched in my code. Only when I tried to make a transaction, the machine denied my request.

"What the hell?"

I reinserted my card and repeated the transaction, being careful to make sure I didn't fat-finger the PIN. Again, the transaction failed. My blood was beginning to boil. While the first time I may have hit a wrong number, I was positive my actions were pristine. I tried a third time, being even more careful than before, slowly and deliberately making sure I touched every key correctly and with the right amount of pressure for it to register. The third attempt at the ATM ended up like the first two, only this time the message "Call Your Processor" flashed on screen.

"I am the processor!" I yelled at the machine.

"What's wrong?" Lynn asked.

"I don't know. It's not working."

"Maybe the card got de-magnetized at the airport or something."

It seemed plausible, although I had never heard of such a feat happening to anyone. Lynn wrapped her arm around me.

"Let's go home," she suggested. "We'll order a pizza and watch a movie."

I felt her reassuring squeeze and placed my arm around her shoulder. We started to walk back in the direction we came. I wasn't going to let this little mishap mess up my evening. If things had looked good before, they were looking even better now.

I felt on top of the world.

Unstoppable.

Little did I know then, but I was wrong.

Dead wrong.

Chapter Thirteen

On the morning of February 11, 2002, I went into the office expecting a routine day. Februarys in Dallas can sometimes fall below freezing, although the average temperature hovers between 67 and 36 degrees Fahrenheit. That day the temperature clung to the upper end of the spectrum, and was warm enough for me to lower the driver's side window and let that cool air freshen up my car.

Carol, our receptionist, called my office the moment I had set my briefcase on the desk and before I had a chance to sip my first cup of coffee. The intercom buzzed, and Carol informed me that there was a man here to see me.

"Who is he, Carol?" I inquired, taking a much needed sip of caffeine. It was not in Carol's nature to be so vague.

"I think you'd better come up front and see for yourself," she replied. There was a tension in her voice, which was rare.

As I entered the waiting area, I was immediately struck by the presence of 20 suit-clad men and women, clutching briefcases, and sitting with unnerved expressions on their faces. Before I could take in the full picture of this moment, an older man stepped forward and flashed a document in my face.

"Mr. Franklin, I am a receiver appointed by the federal courts. The Federal Trade Commission has filed a case against you and your company. I need to speak with you, preferably someplace private." I had never heard the term "receiver" before. A receivership: a court action that places property under the control of a receiver during litigation so that it can be preserved for the benefit of all. A receiver is appointed by a judge after the FTC is able to get an injunction.

If you had asked me what the first words I would hear when I walked into the office the morning of February 11, 2002, "The FTC has filed a case against you" would not have made the list. I started looking for answers to questions that bombarded my mind. How could this be real? On what grounds had they filed a case? Who had complained to the FTC? After what seemed like a minor eternity, I finally found my voice.

"Can I see that document?"

"Of course."

He handed me the document. I thought I might make sense of what was happening if I could at least read and digest the material on the document this stranger was wielding like a weapon.

Before I had even finished the last page of the complaint, the man sputtered into a verbal tirade about the FTC, subpoenas, and serious allegations. While his verbal assault continued, I looked at the faces of my colleagues; there was apprehension on their faces, concern, and confusion. I had no idea what this man was talking about, but for the sake of my employees, I wanted to get these invaders out of the lobby as soon as possible. One thing I had learned in the business world, nothing starts the grind of a rumor mill more than a bunch of business suits perched in your office space like gargoyles.

I looked the older man in the face. There was a cocky glint in his eyes. He was the type of man who not only liked to deliver bad news, but also savored the reaction from his victims.

"Can we talk about this in our conference room?" I asked. "We'll be more comfortable in there, and we can clear up this matter."

Carol showed the interlopers into our conference room. I took this free moment to jet to my office and get a call out to Ross who still hadn't arrived yet. I left him a voicemail, telling him in no uncertain terms that he had to get his ass down to work ASAP because the FTC was breathing down our necks for some reason. I told him to call our lawyers. After I hung up, I scrambled back to the conference room.

"What is this about?" I said, closing the door behind me. Even though I tried to sound as congenial as I could, my voice was edged. The small beads of sweat gathering on my forehead betrayed the anxiety I was feeling. Over and over the same thought beat with my pulse: what could the FTC want with us?

"Mr. Franklin, the FTC has received numerous complaints about your company," the man said.

"Complaints? What complaints? What are you talking about?" My voice was rising with my anger. "Just who are you anyway?"

"I'm Victor Gatling. My team and I have been assigned as receivers. Everything is explained in this portfolio," he said pointing to a thick manila file on the conference room table. "It lists the grievances against your company." He pushed over the file across the table, smirking as he did so. He was a rude one, alright. But he was in the driver's seat. What could I do?

I perused the material as Victor Gatling preached at me. I gathered bits of information along the way in between his incessant droning. Apparently, several of our merchants had accused the company of debiting unexplained funds from their accounts. As I half-listened to Victor, I eerily recalled the previous night when I had stopped by an ATM on my way home to withdraw a few bucks. The machine had refused my card. I had tried a few times, but each time the transaction was rejected. I didn't think anything was wrong at the time. This had happened to a few people I knew. Technology was an imperfect thing. However, now my stomach knotted. The ATM wasn't broken; the FTC had frozen our assets.

I had never felt so helpless as I did sitting there with a gang of FTC thugs, being ambushed with reckless claims I'm sure had no solid foundation.

"Mr. Fanklin," he said again. He loved using my name in an admonishing way. "You have been charged with fraud."

Fraud. The word sent chills up my spine. An allegation of fraud was a serious matter in business, perhaps the most serious. A company's reputation might never recover from the mere whisper of the word; I had seen it happen before firsthand.

"What do you mean, Mr. Gatling?" I had a hard time mustering a polite response for this man. A thousand other sentences crossed my mind, but none of them were kind.

Victor stood in the conference room flanked by two goons: Gary Frederick, his deputy, and Mona Beads, the third in command. It was his way of flexing his muscle, an intimidation technique I'm sure they taught him at FTC 101.

"The allegations are explained in detail in the portfolio, Mr. Franklin. But in a nutshell, several merchants have reported that you misappropriated funds from them. That is a no-no." Victor smirked again. I could tell he was the type of guy that enjoyed pulling the wings off a butterfly.

"I don't understand. Who exactly is making these claims?"

Victor's lips formed a response, but his henchman beat him to the punch.

"Everything's outlined in the portfolio, Mr. Franklin," Frederick said, his voice sounded perturbed the way a parent's might if their kid had asked the same question one too many times. The only thing was, this wasn't just my life and my career at stake, this was a company with over two hundred employees' livelihoods at stake. So what if I asked the same question over and over? And this guy, this Frederick relished the moment almost as much as Victor did. Hell, the three of them in front of me formed a triumvirate of attitude. And they were looking to press me with it until I broke.

Victor, Frederick, Mona Beads, and their henchmen had descended upon the company like a flock of vultures, and like those imposing scavengers, they didn't look like they intended to leave. While I sat down and began reading the portfolio in earnest, they slowly infiltrated ever crevice of our business with the methodical push of a cancer.

As the minutes dragged on to hours, the story came together: 29 of our merchants felt we had hidden fees in our contracts. Incensed, they had informed the FTC of what they termed "unsavory" business practices. We, they argued, had included additional fees in small print throughout the document of which they were unaware. I was stunned. When Ross and I first developed our terms of agreement, we had a prominent Dallas law firm review the contract with a fine-tooth comb. In order to mitigate this exact sort of situation, on the firm's recommendation, we had also added an additional signature on the document that asked the merchant to sign and indicate that the entire document had been read, and all transactions and fees were accepted.

This is not to say that we never had complaints from our merchants. In the past, we had a few problem cases who argued they were being charged fees that they had not agreed to pay. In many cases, we had refunded the fees in order to smooth their ruffled feathers and to continue doing business with important clients. This is not to say we had purposely tried to cheat them; on the contrary, these fees were in accordance to the contract that both parties had signed. We weren't obligated to refund anything; we did so solely for the purpose of pursuing mutual interests. We explained this in painstaking detail to Victor Gatling time and time again throughout this arduous process, but he refused to believe anything we said. Gatling enjoyed having power over others, and he wielded it with the authority and tenacity with which Henry the VIII wielded a leg of mutton; it made him giddy with delight. Under Gatling's stern gaze, I couldn't help but wish we had just reimbursed everyone who had whined about the additional fees; if we had returned the money, we wouldn't be treading water in this nightmare. But as Ross reminded me, no reputable business ever returned fees to complaining clients, especially when there was a legally-binding document attesting to the fact that such a charge was not only legal, it was mandatory. No matter how Victor tried to spin it, we had not done anything legally wrong no matter how many times he wanted to use the word "malfeasance."

For example, some of the merchants complained because we had charged a $400 cancellation fee when merchants broke the terms of our agreement. Our standard contract with each merchant was good for 36 months. If a merchant wanted to get out from under the terms before the three-year period had expired, he was levied with a fee. This was standard practice in the industry, and if you were to ask anyone in the business today, he would tell you the same thing. And here Victor was sitting here telling us that the cancellation charge was fraudulent. It was incredulous.

The FTC reiterated the merchants' claims by criticizing our contract. For one, they argued, all of our fees should have been listed on one page, and not scattered throughout the document. Now, no business document that I have ever read or signed has been organized in this way. Secondly, the FTC informed us that our fees were supposed to be discussed on the first page of the agreement. Again, in all of my years in business, I have never once seen an agreement that followed this practice. Not one single company had an agreement that included all of the fees on the front page, and very few had ever grouped the fees onto a single page. The FTC may be a watchdog of sorts, but they obviously had no business experience themselves. Like many bureaucratic entities, they lived by a "Do what I say, not as I do" philosophy; business degrees didn't equate into business experience. Sometimes, a diploma on the wall is just that – a piece of paper framed professionally by wood and glass.

The FTC maintained its image of self importance as the crusader of the American public, regardless of whether or not they assumed responsibility for themselves to actually do their own homework before getting into something that they couldn't handle. While they talked about taking a clean mop across the industry, in reality, they were targeting solely Ross and me. It was as if there were a separate set of rules that applied to everyone else, and a completely different set for our company. Ross and I spent countless hours trying to pinpoint their motivation. Were they making an example out of us? Were they behind in their quotas? Who knows? But to this day, companies do not list their fees on the first page of their agreements. Every year I check, and every year I see a contract similar to the one that we had used.

As word spread among our employees that Victor and the "Black Suit Gang" (a nickname I had come up with due to their penchant for wearing the same shade of black suits) had assumed control of the company, there was a palpable sense of panic in the air. You could hear the hushed voices sift through the bleak atmosphere and spread into every corner of the office. Would they lose their jobs? Would their bosses go to jail? What are we supposed to do? These questions and more lingered like cold fog. People whispered and would get quiet when one of the Black Suits made a pass by. Tension perched on everyone's shoulder like a bad angel. I felt badly for everyone. This is not what my brother and I sought out to create when we first started. My heart went out to our employees, and it broke seeing them like they were waiting for their name to be called by the executioner.

After a few days, Victor called Ross and I into his office in our building and informed us that it was best if we stayed away while the investigation was ongoing. Part of the reason anxiety was thick was our onsite presence. Given the circumstances, Victor strongly recommended that we leave for everyone's piece of mind.

Ross and I were speechless. Not only had Victor and the Black Suit Gang invaded our office, but now they were horning us out. Essentially, we were being barred from the very business we had created and tended to throughout our adult lives. With one gesture, Victor was in total control.

And he was loving it.

"Go home," he said, as he showed us to the office door. "I'll let you know when you should come back."

Again, he smirked. And with that, the door closed behind us.

Chapter Fourteen

Ross and I retreated to my house and called our lead attorney, Peter Allen. Ross's voice was near frantic on the phone.

"Peter, we've been booted from our company!" Ross said, and he went on to explain the latest developments.

"Hang in there, guys. Rule one: stay out of their way. These pricks know they're in complete control, and they like to flex their muscle. If you fight them on this, you'll only make it worse for yourselves and the company in the long run."

Ross and I didn't like the situation. After all we had done, after all we had accomplished on guts, backing off from a threatening force was not something we were used to doing. But Peter was our lawyer, well versed in the legal intricacies and tactics that the government liked to use. Victor made no bones about telling us to our faces of his intentions; we didn't need to give him or the Black Suit Gang any more ammunition. Nonetheless, we couldn't just relinquish all contact with our company and employees. They were probably clueless, and clueless people had a tendency to make rash decisions. Ross suggested that we ask Victor if we could meet with him weekly to find out what was happening with our business. After several phone calls, Victor reluctantly agreed. Even in dire situations, Ross's penchant for making the hard sale was coming in handy.

Although I was confident in Peter and the rest of our legal team, I continually wondered if Ross and I might have retained some leverage if we'd had a higher profile attorney. Granted, more often than not, those attorneys who represented the majority of clients were not celebrities; they did not possess the name recognition and panache of those who represented the O.J.s of the world. I couldn't help but think that the addition of a person like that would bring media attention on our situation, and that might put pressure on Victor. Anxiety getting the best of me, I sat down and drafted a long e-mail to Alan Dershowitz explaining our case. Afterwards I felt confident that a man of his stature, coupled with his ardent belief of the sanctity of civil liberties, would answer my call for help. I waited for weeks for a response. None ever came.

To compound matters, we had to really watch our money while the investigation lingered at a tortoise pace. It was as if Victor were purposely moving with the precision and speed of a glacier, full well knowing that every day we were losing revenue. While we were not in danger of losing our homes, we were beginning to suffer a cash-flow problem. Many nights I enjoyed the fine cuisine of Raman noodles, which was a far cry from the lifestyle I had developed through the fruits of long hours, working weekends, and putting my nose to the grindstone. While a staple for many students in college, Raman noodles was not filet mignon.

As the weeks wore on, the seizure of the company was the central focus of our lives. Ross and I spent many afternoons in my house shooting pool, which was all we could afford to do, and replayed the moments we could now see with perfect clarity in hindsight that had led to our present predicament.

"We should have refunded those merchants those fees," he said one day, missing a bank shot on the eight ball.

"Yeah, we should have."

"Why didn't you press me on it?"

"I tried. You said it was business."

"It was business."

"And so is where we are now."

Ross stood there, soaking in the moment.

"You know," he said. "I keep thinking about the Texas Attorney General thing."

"Me too."

"What I wouldn't give to get those months back."

Ross was referring to a tête-à-tête we'd had with the Texas Attorney General office several months prior to the FTC's invasion. Some merchants had filed a case with the state concerning our company's fees, but we had ignored their protests because we believed we were justified in levying a charge for breaking our contract. Again, our legal team assured us that our contract was firmly bound within the parameters of the law. The merchants didn't like the fees? Tough. Don't break the contract before its expiration. Still, instead of proactively trying to find an amenable solution to all concerned parties, we had let the situation escalate into a crisis, thinking we were well protected by the law. However, the merchants – and now the FTC – were firmly set that the document was an intentional effort on our part to bleed money from our clients. What we thought was good business they thought was an underhanded and unscrupulous business tactic.

"You can't think like that, Ross," I said, missing my own shot on the eight. "Coulda-woulda-shoulda, the fact remains we didn't. We have to deal with what's in front of us, not howl about what we should have done instead. This is reality, and it's our reality."

Ross didn't say anything. What could he say? He eyed up a shot on the eight and after a few moments of lining up his stick, he struck the white ball. But the shot was imprecise, and it ricocheted badly off the eight sending the white ball hurtling toward the opposite corner pocket for a scratch.

One afternoon over another lackluster pool game, our brother Martin called us. His voice was a combination of panic and incredulousness. Martin had come over to the company a few years earlier after he had gotten out of the Air Force. Martin was a genuinely laid-back kind of person; nothing ever seemed to bother him. He used to tell us stories about boot camp, and how the drill sergeants used to get into his face and try to fluster him. But he just held his ground, bolstered by an inner calmness that is rare in people. He was the only one in his platoon who didn't rattle, who didn't have that breaking point. So, when he had called and shouted expletives into the phone, I had to wonder who the other person on the other end of the line was.

The good news was that Martin was still employed with the company; in fact, none of our employees had been given their pink slips by the FTC. And while Ross and I were concerned that Victor would subject Martin to the same excommunication we had been sentenced to, he either overlooked the family tie, or understood that Martin didn't hold a senior position in the company.

"You sitting down?" Martin asked. I had to pull the phone from my ear because his exuberance was about ten octaves louder than he normally used.

"What's the matter, Martin? What's going on?"

"You aren't going to believe this. Victor is walking around handing out hundred dollar bills to everyone employed by the company. He even sent some guys to the telemarketers."

"What?" I was certain I had misunderstood my brother, or else he had his facts mixed up. There was no way Victor was dishing away that sum of money. A hundred dollars to every employee came to approximately $30,000!

"Is Ross with you? He should hear this too."

I quickly informed Ross of the new development. He took his stick and slammed it down on the pool table, cracking the wood.

"You two need to do something and fast," Martin said. "Victor is out of control."

I quickly hung up with Martin telling him we'd take care of it. We went into my home office and called Victor from the speaker-phone. When Victor answered, Ross exploded.

"Mr. Gatling! What the hell is going on down there?"

"Mr. Franklin, what an unexpected surprise. How are you doing?"

"Dispense with the formalities and answer the damn question, Victor! You're robbing my family of everything we have worked for. Who gave you the right to hand out our money without our approval?"

"Under the circumstances, employee morale at your company is, well, lacking. I think that a little pick-me-up would go far to assuage their fears and uncertainties."

"If you think hundred dollar tips are in order, why don't you dig into your own pocket? After all, at a pay rate of four hundred dollars an hour, you should have a few bucks to spare!"

I wish I could say that was the only disturbing information we received regarding Victor's unorthodox practices, but it wasn't. Two of Victor's assistants were overheard discussing how they been paid a bonus to urinate on the roof of the building.

I am not kidding.

They were paid to urinate. I couldn't make this stuff up if I tried.

But wait, there's more.

Apparently, Gary Frederick was working a second job on the side to his primary responsibilities of tearing through our office records. Frederick was billing us for eight hours of work per day, five days per week, so Ross and I wondered how he had the time to work another job. My family and I were eating egg noodles for dinner, and Frederick was milling us for our children's inheritance.

Ross confronted Frederic about his bogus time card. He had an elaborate explanation, of course, a work of fiction that even Hemingway would be proud of. According to Frederick, he went to work at six a.m., worked for eight full straight hours without a lunch break (yeah, right), and then drove to his second job where he worked late into the evening. We weren't in a position to question him, even though we knew his "supposed" schedule was a blatant lie. Again, here Ross and I were under the microscope for our perceived lack of ethics, and this guy was cheating the clock on our dime! But while we knew the truth, we didn't have the concrete proof from which to make an official complaint, so we were forced to continue to pay him, knowing full well he was bleeding us dry.

But wait, there's still more.

As bad as Frederick's bloated time card was, it did not even come close to being the receivership's most flagrant violation.

At the annual national convention for our industry in Las Vegas that year, Victor, Frederick, and Mona Beads attended as representatives for our company!

Preposterous? Yes. Absolutely true? I will swear on a stack of Bibles.

When the triumvirate returned, they made no bones about talking about their adventures in Sin City around some of our employees. Apparently, Victor and company had a meeting there with one of our chief competitors. And get this – the three of them had discussed selling our company's private records to this major competitor. Essentially, all the secrets of our business were up for grabs to the highest bidder. Eventually months later when this whole sordid affair ended and Victor's long dark shadow had been lifted from the company, Ross and I discovered a proposal Frederick had written to the competitor that quoted six million dollars as the asking price for our business secrets. Now remember, and this is important, the receivership – *any* receivership – is supposed to preserve the company's assets while the legal wrangling takes place. However, *our* receivers, the supposed guardians of our business, were conspiring against us, ripping us off, and trying to make millions off the knowledge we'd spent years learning.

Ethical? I dare you to find any shred of ethics.

"We have to fix that jerk," Ross said to me, after learning of the triumvirate's trip to Vegas.

"I'd love to, but we're under the microscope. We can't butt heads with Victor."

"He's taking food off our table! First, he gave away our money, and then he paid Tweedle Dee and Tweedle Dum to piss on us. What's next? Systematically breaking apart the company and selling it off?"

"I know. I feel the same as you do. But you heard what Peter said. If we provoke him, it might get worse."

"Jesus, what can be worse than this?" Ross asked. My brother was frustrated, and so was I. But there was nothing we could do. "Look, we both know he's purposely running the company into the ground. We have got to be able to do something. It won't be worth two nickels after he's through running his filthy fingers through it. He's supposed to be the receiver, for crying out loud! He's supposed to preserve the company's best interests, not run them into the ground."

Ross and I knew that there was little hope of voicing our concerns to Victor. He was a man on a mission. Compounding matters was the fact that Frederick seemed just as crooked as Victor was. We did, however, think that Mona Beads could be a potential ally in this fiasco. We decided to approach her, and made sure we were away from the prying eyes of the rest of the Black Suit Gang. Mona agreed to have lunch with us.

At the restaurant, Mona was cordial, as she had always been, but she seemed a bit on edge. Ever the businessman, Ross got directly to the point and immediately told her what we had heard.

"Mona, let's be frank here. We know for a fact that when you went to Vegas for the convention, you, Victor, and Frederick met with our competitors."

Mona's face flushed. Obviously, she was taken aback by not only Ross's candor, but also by the fact that we seemed to know what transpired.

"I don't know what you're talking about, Ross," she stuttered. I wish I could have played poker with this woman. She couldn't bluff to save her life.

"Cut the crap, Mona," Ross interjected. "You're not Victor or Frederick. I expect to get the run-around from them. I thought you had more character than the rest of your colleagues. Maybe I was wrong."

Ross gave me the sign and we got up to leave. Mona hesitated a second then capitulated. Ross had played his hand very well.

"Sit down," Mona said.

Ross and I sat back down. Mona leaned in close.

"Listen, the meeting in Vegas is not what you think," she said.

"Pardon me for not believing you quite yet," Ross replied. "Word on the street has it you met with our competitors and offered to sell them everything you've learned about our business operation."

"It's not like that," was all Mona could say.

"Then how is it exactly? You sell our secrets, you'll cripple us. We have people here, loyal employees, Mona, that will be out of jobs if you take apart this company."

Mona let out a long, exasperated sigh, dropping her hands onto her lap

"Okay, Ross, I understand why you are so angry. And yes, in my opinion, it's wrong, but I didn't arrange that meeting. It was Victor's plan start to finish. I was as blindsided then as you are now. One minute we're talking with some other industry professionals, the next he's gone down the dark path of selling your business profile. I know you're in a tight spot, but I'm not exactly sitting in the catbird seat."

Mona's face got very serious. She leveled her eyes directly at mine.

"Look, I think what Victor did was appalling. His face makes my skin crawl if you want to get right down to it. But the bottom line is, like the cliché says, it's business. Not the right way of doing it in my opinion, but business nonetheless."

"Why didn't you stand up for us?" Ross asked.

"What could I do, Ross? What would you have done in my position? And before you answer altruistically, think about the fact that you're not the only ones with real life concerns. I have no control over Victor. He can wreck my career too. You're not the only ones that have to worry about their families."

"The only thing different, Mona, is that he's affecting more than one family with our company," I said, chiming in on the conversation. "He's affecting over two hundred."

"And I'm sorry about that," she said sincerely. "When the meeting took place, I couldn't believe what I was hearing. And then, when we got back, I couldn't very well say anything because of professional repercussions."

"Great, Mona," Ross said rising from the table. "You have a bastard in charge, and all of his flunkies won't say anything because they are afraid to get their hands slapped."

"We're all not lucky enough to be our own bosses, Ross. Some of us have to actually work for another person," Mona said coolly as she watched my brother storm out of the restaurant.

When we left lunch that day, Ross and I both realized that our problems with Victor and the receivership had escalated to the point that could no longer be ignored. It was one thing for the FTC to conduct their investigation; however, it was quite another thing to stand by and watch the receivers break every law in the book. Something had to be done, and it was time for action. There was little choice left in the matter. Ross and I kept coming to the same conclusion: it was time for our attorneys to contact the FTC and make them aware of the receivers' conduct.

We called Peter Allen and informed him that Mona had practically confessed to Victor's meeting with the competitor. If it were possible to hear drool coming out of someone's mouth on the other end of a phone, I could hear our attorney salivating at this new development. After about a twenty minute conversation, Peter believed we had enough evidence to make an official request to replace the receivers for the duration of the investigation. Peter made sure he had all of his documents ready, prepared his legal arguments, and felt better than 70 percent that the FTC would re-move Victor and the Black Suit Gang.

The FTC's reply?

Settle the case and they would remove the receivers. Until the case reached some sort of conclusion, the receivers would remain where they were.

You got to love the government.

Now, before I move on, let's just take this moment to ponder the FTC's decision to keep the receivership in place. Under the guise of their mission statement, the FTC was the lead federal organization in charge of preserving justice, "righting the wrongs" of the U.S. business community, and proponents of truth, justice, and the American way (Okay, that's Superman, but my interactions with agents of the FTC during this time period have shown that they have a very high opinion of themselves). And yet, despite this pageantry, they were the people blackmailing us! According to the FTC, our entire company was corrupt to the core, but they were the ones not above using muscle to get what they wanted from us: a settlement. They were not interested in getting to the root of the matter; they, like other federal entities whose budgets depended on meeting quarterly and yearly quotas, were looking to pad their statistics. The FTC's callousness deeply offended Ross and me. They didn't care whether or not our company survived; rather, they were doing all they could to see it destroyed so that they could proudly state afterwards: "We took on corporate America for the small guys and won."

❧

"I tell you what we need to do," Ross said to me one day as we were driving through Dallas. "We need to dig up some dirt on Victor. See if we can't flex our own muscle."

"I think we know enough already," I said. "He's an ass."

"I mean something more scandalous. Something that might hurt him if it's brought into the public eye."

"Like what?"

"Everyone has a weakness, and that's usually tied to a secret. We look hard enough and we might just find his."

"He's a robot," I groaned. "He's like T-2 – only more annoying than the originally version. You've seen him strut around the office, beating his chest like some ape in the jungle. Always drawing attention to himself."

"That's it!" Ross exclaimed.

"He's an ape?"

"No, you said it yourself. He likes to brag about his accomplishments. He always puffs himself up, flashing his colored feathers like a peacock."

"Okay, I'm still not following you, Ross."

"Well, if we were to ask the right questions, who's to say he won't blurt out something incriminating? Think about it. He's always so quick to take the credit for something, to boost his image in front of everyone else that he might not realize what he's saying. We get it down, or have someone hear him say that, we may actually have some room to maneuver."

"I don't know. He hates us. You think he'd let his guard down like that?"

"I'm counting on his hatred. Don't you see? He wants us to see what a big deal he is. He wants you and me to know that he has raised himself from nothing to the middle-management echelon of the mighty FTC. He's in competition with us; he always has been from the moment he walked through our doors. He relishes his position right now because he thinks that makes him a success. I'm telling you, he'll blurt out something bad if we push the right buttons."

As Ross spoke, his voice rose in excitement to a level I hadn't seen since this ordeal started. For the first time in a long time, Ross had his piss and vinegar back. It was good to see my brother like that, if even for a moment.

"How do you propose we do this, Ross?"

My brother smiled at me.

Ross was back.

❧

I have to hand it to my brother; despite everything that had happened, he hadn't lost his prowess for business. He devised an elaborate "cloak and dagger" routine where I was to wear a tape recorder whenever we met with Victor so that we would have a running record of all of our conversations, and of course, of any indiscretions that he may let slip. Before our next meeting with Victor, I hooked a small microphone to the t-shirt I wore underneath my button-down Oxford and slipped the cassette recorder into the front pocket of my khakis.

I purposely sat next to Victor and leaned into the conversation so the microphone could pick up his words. I must admit, I was damned nervous that first time with the recorder. I now have a greater appreciation for undercover police officers who must wear wires to get evidence. It's truly a high-anxiety position to be in. Sitting there listening to Victor speak, all I could think of was: How does he not know? I could feel the pulse in my neck pounding out a heavy drumbeat rhythm. As he droned on, I wondered if Victor hadn't bugged my house and listened to everything that Ross and I had been saying about him. There was nothing below Victor. He'd stoop to any level to maintain his position in the pecking order.

At the end of the meeting, Ross and I waited until we got to his car before we made any mention of how the undercover operation went. We tried to look as calm and collected as we always did, but the anticipation of the moment sped us quickly into the car.

"Well? How did it go?" Ross asked once we pulled out of the parking lot.

"Unproductive. The bastard didn't say anything incriminating."

Ross's face deflated.

"What did he say?"

"How the heck should I know? He just jabbered on about things. I'm telling you, Ross, my heart was jumping a mile a minute. I could barely concentrate."

"Maybe next time will be better," he said.

"Next time, you wear the mic."

"I can't. I'd get so mad at him, we'd go at it, and the meeting would be over. Besides, you're perfect for espionage. You don't let your emotions get in the way of the mission. You're like... you're like the James Bond of Texas."

"Very funny."

"You were especially good when you craned your neck there at the beginning, trying to point that damn microphone in Victor's direction."

"Oh, God. You saw that?"

Ross was chuckling now.

"I was afraid Victor would think you were trying to plant one on his cheek. He might have filed for sexual harassment." Ross cracked up.

"Oh, you are just hilarious."

"Imagine bringing him over to Mom's for dinner."

"My sides are splitting," I said dryly.

"Who's going to be best man? Me or Martin?"

We drove back to my home the rest of the way, Ross dropping one-liners. In retrospect, it was the perfect tension breaker for the day. Afterwards I'd agree to give the hidden mic operation another try, and my brother and I embraced, the way only brothers can do.

I met Lynn at Joseph's later that evening. I was almost two hours late, and when I walked inside, I found her sitting at the table, the drink in front of her untouched, the ice cubes having long since melted.

"I'm sorry," I said, sitting in the chair across from her.

She didn't acknowledge me at first. I could tell from the look on her face that she had been thinking about something for a while and had finally arrived at some sort of decision, which I was about to hear.

"The attorney ran over," I explained. "He went over all of our options. Ross wants to fight this to the end, and – "

"Stop it," she said. "Just stop it, Adam. Okay?"

"What's the matter?" I said. "I was just a bit late."

"What's wrong? The question isn't 'what's wrong,' it's 'what isn't wrong?'" She sighed and looked away gathering her thoughts. "I mean, how did we get here? How did things get to the place where we are at right now?

She wasn't hysterical. Her voice was steady, void of any tonal inflection or emotion. That worried me. People are only emotionless when they've reached the end of their rope, when they've considered all of the options in front of them, and after careful self-scrutiny for better or for worse, decided upon a course of action.

"Lynn," I said trying to alleviate the tension that had dug a trench between us. "It's a tough time right now. Christ, the FTC is camped out in our building. Can we just put this on hold for right now?"

"There is only 'right now,' Adam. That's what I'm trying to tell you. 'Later' is for other people."

"Wait – what are you saying?"

"You're right. The FTC is camped at your building. You have to concentrate on that. I understand, really I do. You've built something special from the ground up, and now there's some monster trying to bring it down with a wrecking ball. I can't imagine what that feels like, to have someone barge in wanting to take all that you have worked for. But that's not the only thing being destroyed, Adam. The thing between us, our relationship, that's also being destroyed. And that's something I can imagine because I'm feeling it every day when you're absent from me both physically and emotionally. And that's something I can't bear."

She paused a moment to see if I would say anything. I didn't. I couldn't. After the day I had just experienced, this was the last thing in the world that I expected or needed.

"I can't play second team to your business any more, Adam. I won't."

"It'll get better," I managed. It was a lame response, but I was desperate. I had to say something even if it wasn't the right thing. And it wasn't. I know because she looked at me the way you look at a puppy when he's done something so pathetically stupid.

"I've heard that song before, and I know the words by heart. You can't change who you are, Adam. I think part of you wants to, but there's another part, and that part is stronger."

"Are you saying what I think you're saying?" I said.

"You're a good person. You have limitless potential. The things I've seen in you are wonderful. You just haven't learned to figure out what's important to you – what really matters to you –

and what isn't. Until you take the time to work that out, you'll always find yourself in these situations."

She stood up from the table.

"I want the best for you, Adam," she continued. "I hope it all works out the way you want."

With that, she left. I sat there speechless, staring at her untouched cocktail. It was like someone had taken a sledgehammer to my stomach, and I was trying to desperately get my wind back.

Relationships – gotta love them.

My next meeting with Victor, I wore the mic again, but this time I was more relaxed and less like a spy-in-training. We talked, and I was forced to listen to Victor's profound philosophies on life. In the end, he said nothing incriminating that we could use for leverage against him and the Black Suit Gang.

"We need a better strategy," I lamented to Ross after the second operation failed to yield positive results.

"We have to find a way to get him talking at length about his other cases," Ross planned.

For the next couple of hours, Ross and I started to devise a plan to get Victor to spill his guts. We hashed out a good plan, to get Victor on the defensive and hammer away at him together until his frustration got so high, that he would be forced to talk.

Unfortunately, we never had a chance to implement that course of action. Our attorneys had a plan, and even though we wanted desperately to try our way, Peter Allen convinced us that the best way to fight the legal machine of the government was with legal tactics.

Ross and I were anxious to go on the offensive. We just wanted to get back to our company and start to put the pieces back that Victor had broken off. Our attorneys told us that they thought the case could be settled, which relieved Ross and me. This ordeal had dragged out too long, and Lord knows how much money the company had lost due to Victor's feet-dragging. Our attorneys proposed that we make some changes to our merchant's agreement, work with customer service to ensure customer satisfaction, and pay the FTC a substantial fine of one million dollars. While that sum was enough to make anyone blink, the fact remained that to get things back to the way they used to be was worth any amount of money.

Ross and I left Peter Allen's offices with a sense of relief. For the first time in weeks, we genuinely smiled at what the future could bring. But before the day was over, our high spirits would plummet once again.

That evening, Ross was at my home for what we thought was a celebratory dinner when Peter Allen called. I expected him to tell me the FTC had accepted our offer, and the receivers would evacuate our office immediately.

We didn't hear that response.

"Listen…" there was a hesitance to Peter that caused a flood of panic to wash over me. "They are not going to do this fairly. They want it all."

"All? What do you mean 'all'?"

"The company. The assets. Everything."

"Can they do that?"

"I'm afraid so. They want to liquidate the company. They're making you guys an example."

I hung up on Peter. I knew I had to talk to him, to talk though this situation, but I couldn't right then. There was a more pressing thing I had to take care of. I had to figure out a way to tell my brother that our company was on the chopping block.

Ross could tell from my reaction that the call had not gone the way we had anticipated.

As I explained the FTC's demands, Ross's face registered the gamut of emotions: terror, anger, fear, sadness.

"What about the three hundred people we have working for us, who rely on our company to pay their mortgages, their bills, the kids' tuitions? This is bigger than just the two of us. What about them?"

"What can I say? They aren't thinking of them, Ross. They want to destroy us, destroy what two guys without a college education built with sweat and a vision. That's what they're after."

Ross took a deep breath. I knew that he had come to a decision standing there those few minutes.

"We're not going to let this thing die without a fight. If we go out, we go out kicking and screaming."

"And take some bodies with us."

"At least Victor."

"At least Victor," I agreed. "Remember the time when you bought your Integra and we left our golf clubs in your old Buick you traded in?"

"Yeah, I remember."

"And we went back to the dealership to get them back, and they told us they didn't have them."

"Stealing bastards."

"And what did we do? We took them to court. We were so sure the judge would side with us because we were the ones telling the truth. We were convinced that we would win, remember? Because we were right. And what happened?"

"The judge hosed us."

"The judge didn't rule in our favor. And what did we learn?"

"That being in the right isn't enough."

A moment of silence settled between us as we both pondered our first experiences inside a U.S. courtroom.

"We haven't changed much since then," I said finally. "We are in this mess now because we believed, just like we did when we were kids, that telling the truth is enough."

"So we're idealistic. How is that supposed to make me feel any better?" Ross said.

"We aren't idealistic. We just play by the rules and expect others to do the same. Bottom line, Ross: there are people out there who just don't play fair. And they're not just regular people, but the government as well."

Ross smiled. "I guess you're right. We haven't changed."

"A bit older maybe."

He laughed. It was good to hear that sound from my brother.

"Ross, we've had more success than anyone I know. We've had charmed lives if you think about it. And we didn't screw over anyone to get to where we are now. Regardless of what happens, at least we can sleep knowing that, not only did we make our own lives better, we made three hundred other people's lives better as well."

Ross nodded his head in silence.

The die was cast. We would fight this losing battle. The same drive that had led us to climb the ladder of success would now be channeled in fighting a system hell-bent on destroying us. I couldn't help but think of King Leonidas in the Battle of Thermopylae. Three hundred Spartans might have lost the battle, but they won a much bigger war.

Chapter Fifteen

No matter how much time passes, I am always struck by the hypocrisy of the FTC. Ross and I were portrayed as double-crossing swindlers, con men out to steal money from legitimate hardworking businesses. And yet, the FTC was the real thief, the one who wanted to smash apart our company with a sledgehammer and sell off the pieces to the highest bidder. They were determined to milk us for every cent we had ever made, for every dollar we were worth, with the ultimate goal of bankrupting my brother and me. There was absolutely no precedent in the industry for the kind of treatment to which we were subjected. But throughout it all, the FTC maintained this moral high ground as saviors of the oppressed. It was sickening.

Regardless of our distaste for them, the FTC was in reality a vicious adversary, bankrolled by the U.S. Government. They had time on their side, and perhaps more important, they had the full power and support of the legal system. Not for a single moment could we lose sight of their abilities. They could pull all of the necessary strings on their behalf. I couldn't help but think of poor old Don Quixote, futilely tilting at the windmill. The only difference between us and him was that he had no idea that he would lose, for us, the possibility loomed over us like a bad angel.

Ross and I met with our legal team at their Dallas office for a marathon meeting to save our company. The meeting lasted the entire day, from noon until the following noon. During this time, we fiercely brainstormed possible solutions only to disregard one after the other. Finally, at the end of that twenty-four hour period, we finally developed an offer that the FTC might accept: we doubled our offer to two million dollars, and included a detailed summary of our own grievances. We cited our frustration that we appeared to be the only company that had been targeted, when there were numerous companies that had routinely engaged in the same business practices. Despite our attorney's objections, we had one question that we wanted the FTC to answer: Why hadn't they included those other companies in the suit?

At my house, Ross and I regrouped and waited for the FTC to respond. We tried to kill time by shooting pool, watching t.v., and playing cards. Nothing could take our minds off the situation. It was like a prisoner on death row waiting to hear if he was going to be granted last second clemency by the governor.

After a few hours, the FTC called us. This time, they acknowledged that we had made some valid points about the industry. In light of this, they were going to go easy on us. They only wanted half of our company.

I couldn't make this up if I tried.

Half the company. What an offer. I only felt *half* as sick as I had before.

In addition, they informed us that negotiations were over. We were to take the offer or leave it; settle or prepare for court. They left it up to us.

To say that my brother and I were livid would be a grave understatement. The entire company – half the company – for something that was not against the law - it was unfathomable. In either case, we would lose our company. The only other option we had was to engage in a long, costly court battle.

Settle and lose the very essence of what we had created, or fight the imposing ogre that was, and still is, the federal government.

Fight it was.

In due time, I received my subpoena. I was at home when the doorbell rang and this guy that looked like a used car salesman thrust the paper into my chest.

"Have a good day," he said and bolted out of there.

I did not look forward to testifying, but I had nothing to hide. We were in the right, and maybe the contract could have been organized better, but the fact remained that it was a legitimate contract that was standard in our industry.

I spent the course of five grueling days with our attorneys preparing for my questioning. Peter Allen asked me questions from every angle. No question was too tough or too irrelevant. He and his team bombarded me, assuming an attacking style then a more compassionate one. He didn't want me to be caught off guard. He had seen federal attorneys before; some were hacks, but some were very good and could have earned two times their GS salaries at a private firm. At the end of my "Testimony Bootcamp," I was ready for my showdown with David Foxx, the FTC's lead counsel. Peter got me the 411 on Foxx, and it was not a favorable draw. While not the best sharpshooter in the FTC arsenal, he was good enough and had tallied several notches on his prosecutor's bedpost. As I waited for the deposition to begin, I reviewed the coaching I had received from my attorneys: take my time, don't let Foxx rattle me with offbeat questions, and above all, tell the truth.

Finally, judgment day arrived. I remember walking up to the courthouse that morning. Like so many Dallas mornings, it was clear and cool, with just the hint of the approaching heat accenting the air. It would be a hot one later to be sure, but at that moment, it was like the calm before the storm. Nonetheless, it was my chance to tell our side of the story. If nothing else, I was going to put the truth on the record. Walking up the steps, ignoring reporters' questions, I thought I had glimpsed Lynn hanging out on the fringe of the crowd of spectators gathered on the street. Between the microphones being thrust in my face and the cacophony of questions fired at me, I couldn't be certain if it was her or someone else. If it was her, I thought that it could be a good sign of the things to come. This wasn't to be the case.

The deposition was long. Very long.

For two days, Foxx hammered me. His questions were like a boxer's punches, a series of hard and soft combinations that came at me from all directions. As Peter predicted, he'd try to set me up, and then follow a relatively irrelevant question with a haymaker, trying to decapitate me in one fell swoop. He'd ask me a number of outlandish questions that I couldn't have possibly have known: if I didn't know an answer or didn't have a response to one, he'd make it seem like I was dim-witted. When I responded promptly, he went after it like a junkyard dog on a soup bone. With his partly redundant, partly ridiculous line of questioning, there was little doubt that Foxx was doing his best to bait me. I thank Peter for those days in preparation; if it were not for those painstaking hours, I would have lost my cool.

Midway through the second day, Foxx was visibly frustrated. There is little doubt that Foxx had expected me to break during his onslaught. He wanted me to confess that Ross and I were traveling snake oil salesmen whose contract was the magic elixir made to bilk merchants out of their money. But I kept proclaiming the truth. We had taken every precaution to create a viable, understandable agreement that had been gone over by a legal team well versed in the mechanics of drafting contracts in our industry. It was a cogent legal document, and if there were any problems with it, it certainly could not be with the legal base.

After my testimony, the negotiations seemed to move a bit quicker. The FTC came forward with an obscene sum of money for a settlement, an amount that would have crippled us. Our team fired back with a counteroffer, and the FTC returned with a smaller but still hefty settlement amount. It was like two old warships going broadside and letting each other have it with their cannons. The negotiations went back and forth without end. But each time the FTC came back with a smaller amount. When the smoke finally cleared, the FTC's final offer was a manageable sum with the admonition that if we didn't pay it, the next time we'd see them would be in a court in front of a judge.

Peter informed us that it was impossible to win against the FTC in federal court. If we fought them, we'd lose. An entity like the FTC was established to win battles in court; they couldn't lose, because if they did, the American public, as well as the federal government, would wonder why such an agency existed.

Ross and I had some heavy decisions to make. We knew we could sell the company, pay the fine, and have plenty left to provide comfortable lives for our families. We'd have millions to reinvest, keeping the dream alive to own our own sports franchise someday. But we had planned to provide outstanding retirement plans for those who had helped us build the company. If we paid the sum, we'd have to renegotiate those retirements, and that was an awful proposition. Loyalty is priceless in this world, and it deserves to be rewarded in any way possible.

The one sticking point that annoyed me to no end is that no matter how many times we had said it, the FTC failed to acknowledge that we had done nothing that wasn't an accepted and regular practice in our industry. And never once did they acknowledge our grievances against the receivership. All that had been swept under a long bureaucratic rug of red tape.

Bottom line: the only way to get rid of the receivership and put this to an end was settle with the FTC.

I couldn't help but picture Don Quixote limping away from the windmill, his lance broken, and Sancho riding behind him singing a sad, sad song.

Chapter Sixteen

We had to sell our company. Period.

My brother and I decided to meet with a prominent firm who specialized in selling companies like ours. As was par for the course with our rise from independent start-up to commercial success, we channeled our friends' assistance. Ross had a high school buddy named David who worked for this firm. Then we sent out letters of introduction to over fifty companies who might be interested in acquiring our business. As we predicted, many of them were very interested. We ended up narrowing it down to five serious offers and soon met with each of them in Dallas. One group in particular flew all the way from Puerto Rico with a group of twelve representatives. They were part of a large bank, and we thought that bringing in the whole team was indication that they were very serious. Initially, Ross and I were excited by the prospect and the attention as another validation that we had created a monumental success. However, after a few days of negotiating, they backed off, offering less than was principally on the table. In the end, we turned them down. Over the next couple of weeks, Ross and I met with the representatives of each one of these potential candidates from four to six hours. Each time was a varied version of the same dog and pony show, complete with colorful prospectuses and power point presentations. It was interesting to learn how so many groups did not have a serious interest in buying. It was amazing how they had succeeded in their respective fields. And these weren't local companies; some flew from all over the country looking for a fantastic liquidation sale. Ross and I were more than a bit surprised how this really only came down to two companies out of around fifty-five who actually had a serious offer to complement their serious interest.

After several months of doing this song and dance, Ross and I ended up selling our company to an investment firm out of New York. They had just purchased a competitor of ours in Fort Worth and planned to merge the two. To be honest, it wasn't the best or most lucrative offer, and under better circumstances, we'd have made a lot more, but the deal did finally enable us to settle our case with the FTC. Although it was a huge relief to see the end of this nightmare, it was also deeply disheartening. We knew we had been railroaded and our hand had been forced. Still, there was nothing we could do.

As you can imagine by now, Ross and I have never been personalities who enjoyed relinquishing the reins of control so easily. We had always believed that we had the power to make our lives what we wanted them to be. Not unlike Benjamin Franklin, we were truly self-made men who had risen to the heights they had achieved via hard work, sweat, and a vision of what things could be. All our lives had proven this to be true... until that moment the FTC walked into our lives. Helplessness is not an emotion that my brother and I naturally took to. However, I had to accept that the final leg of our journey was not a part of our original plan; we had been coerced down this road by powers greater than us, and when the smoke finally cleared from the field of battle, I had to own up to that.

I can't speak for Ross, but for me the pivotal moment transpired the day that phone call came from Peter Allen.

"They want it all," he said. And with those words, I knew that the company was lost. I knew the FTC would not relent until Ross and I went out of the business. I never asked Ross if he had come to the same conclusion; it is one of those instances where the answer – any answer – wouldn't satisfy the question being asked.

All along, I had worried about what would happen to my brother when the moment finally came and the company left our hands. In all honesty, during the process I had slowly come to grips with the situation, and inside I started to distance myself from the company. But Ross was another matter. While we were both own-ers, he was the true brains and visionary behind it all. And even though he never said anything outright, I knew that signing those papers had to be as painful as a dagger to the heart. Thankfully, an opportunity came about that softened the blow a bit.

Ever the salesman, Ross had negotiated the sale to allow him to retain a position in the new company. He would be in charge of spearheading the new company's growth, which was his natural strength. While a prouder man may have thumbed his nose at the offer, it was important to Ross that he maintained some connection to the company that he had birthed and raised into one of the finest in the industry. Ross would have been unable to walk away and leave completely; like the parable of King Solomon and the baby, Ross would rather see his baby intact with another mother than to see it divided.

Ross's inclusion was valuable for another reason, too. We still had to achieve our earn-out, which is an additional payment an acquired company receives after the merger, based on their pro-jected future earnings. Our earn-out had been determined, and it all hinged on the company reaching a target number of accounts. If the new company met the target goal, we'd collect a multi-million dollar earn-out. With Ross still involved, it was all but certain that the target would be met. Let's face it, even though the FTC had taken our company and left us hurting, they hadn't diminished our business savvy; we still knew how to turn a profit! They couldn't destroy the impulse, the *drive* that we possessed; we became successful on our determination to succeed, not because someone handed it to us in the first place.

Here's a lesson in Business 101: in any deal, there are always bumps along the way; nothing ever transpires without some turbulence, some unseen obstacle that suddenly rears its ugly head in your path. Of course, this transaction was especially trying because of the chain of events that had brought it into existence in the first place. Before we were able to finalize our merger, we got some turbulence from an unlikely source of all places, and fate dealt us one last cold affront.

As part of the sale, the new company would acquire our top three executives: Blain, Rich, and Harry. All three had agreed to sign employment agreements guaranteeing that they would join the new business and help get it off and running. One afternoon, Blain, our Chief Financial Officer, called Ross and requested a meeting with the three executives, as well as Ross and me. At the meeting, Blain explained that there were some issues that needed to be addressed.

The three executives explained that they wanted increases in salary and informed us that they were not going to sign the employment agreements unless that point was taken care of. If it wasn't, they wanted to be free to start their own company, and therefore could not be tied into a new company by the agreement.

"So you see, guys, this might prevent us from closing the deal," Ross said after he went through the situation. It was easy to see that Blain had been elected spokesperson for the other two. It was a role he relished, as he was trying hard not to let his smile crease his "professional" face.

I don't want to tell you how badly I wanted to punch Blain in the head. After all we had done for him; here he was making a power play. These guys were supposed to be our best friends, our extended family, given every opportunity available to them; now, it was like all of that was out the window. They didn't seem to care what happened to us.

"Look," Ross said. "I understand that you want to start your own company. You guys are smart. You learned a lot and are anxious to get out there and see what you can do on your own. My brother and I support that. We only ask that you don't do anything to mess up our deal. It's not like we have many options on the table. And if I remember, when we brought you on, you didn't have many options either."

Blain and the others avoided his look.

"How about this," Ross continued. "Sign the agreement, work for them until your non-compete expires, and then start your own company. But just sign the agreement."

There was a moment of silence as the three "executives" sat there. I could almost see the cogs turning in Blain's head.

"Okay, Ross. But what about the other thing we're here for. The salaries. I mean, come on, without a substantial raise, we'd be forced to quit."

"Hold on here," I interrupted. I couldn't control my anger any longer. "Let's get something straight. Do you want to start your own company, or do you want raises?"

"Both."

My expression must have given away what I was feeling because Blain interjected before I could respond.

"You know, this just didn't happen to you two," Blain said. "Our entire team at the company was affected by the FTC case. We are just trying to look out for ourselves now, to get what's ours. You'd do the same."

Ross stopped me before I said anything else.

"We'll get back to you," Ross said.

And with that we rose from our chairs, and walked out of the room.

Just when you think it's over, there's always something else. This was our something else.

For the next several days, Huey, Dewey, and Louie (my not-so-flattering nickname for our former friends) continued to press for higher salaries or else quit, which would undoubtedly complicate, and maybe even quell, the merger. Their purpose was clear: they intended to extort us. They would hold their involvement with the new company over our heads to force us to cough up huge sums of money. Ross and I discussed whether or not the company could survive without them on board. Part of me didn't care; I wanted them to hit the streets and stop feeding off the company tit. Ross was in accordance; he wanted to fire them all, to call their bluff, but with our company's sale in the balance there was really no way out of it. Deep down, neither one of us wanted to take that gamble. Too much was at stake, and too much had already happened. The fight was out of both of us.

I just want to go on record and say that all of my years in corporate America hadn't prepared me for the backstabbing we were getting from Blain, Rich, and Henry. Although Blain had been a professional success in his own right when he asked to join us, Rich and Harry had been waiters and bartenders prior to joining our team and enjoying the fruits of our success. Now, understand, I make no offense to waiters and bartenders. It's good honest work. But those professions do not provide the kind of lifestyles that Dewey and Louie had been living. And they had acquired managerial experience in a hot bustling industry that would open doors for them throughout their lives. Ross and I had even given Blain numerous personal loans over the years, no questions asked. Now, none of that seemed to matter. Ross and I were no longer friends to them; we were an opportunity to make a buck. They were treating us just as insensitively as the FTC had. And it made me sick.

It made Ross sicker, because he held out; he was convinced they would eventually buckle and sign the agreement. When he spoke to them next, he said to me, he would assert that we couldn't swing a raise no matter how much pressure was applied. In the end, Ross's perseverance won out. The three reluctantly signed their agreements as was promised, but the damage was done personally. You can't heal wounds that have been ripped open with a crowbar. Since that tense period, we have never spoken to any of them. Good luck, and good riddance.

With the agreements signed, the deal went through, and the company was officially absorbed into its new home. For the first time since I was twenty-one and Ross was a mere teenager, we didn't have our own company to run.

Epilogue

I saw Lynn one night a week after the agreement was signed. I went into Joseph's alone. I was tired of being by myself and tired of talking about the business with Ross. I needed to get away, step outside the problem that was my life and just be in a place that didn't ask any questions.

Maybe part of me expected to see her there, but I don't think so.

She was there in back shooting pool by herself. It was good to see her again after so much time had elapsed since she gave me my walking papers. She was eyeing up shots like she had when I first saw her. The familiar crack of ball against ball was almost comforting.

I walked into the back and watched her combo the five-ball into the side pocket. After she made the shot, she looked up at me.

Our eyes met in a visual embrace, except there was no awkwardness, no self-consciousness that typically accompanied such an act.

"You here to play or stare?" she asked me.

"You want some competition?"

"I don't know. Are you competition?"

"I can handle a stick," I replied, smiling.

"I don't need to know what you do on a Friday night."

She went back to measuring the angles on a possible shot.

"How are you, Lynn?"

She checked the angles. "I'm good. Real good. And you?"

"Fine."

"Everything get resolved?" she asked, as she positioned herself to shoot.

"We sold the company."

"Good for you. You must have made a lot of money."

"I don't care about that," I said. And for the first time in my life, I knew I meant it.

"Well, maybe you learned something after all."

"More than you know."

It must have been the sincerity in my voice, because Lynn stopped before she shot and stood up from her leaning position.

"Now that's interesting. I'm all ears."

"You told me, Lynn. You were talking, but I wasn't hearing you."

"Yeah, well sometimes the smartest people in the world don't listen."

"Show me where they are. I think I'll buy them a drink."

She smiled. And that's when I left it all on the table.

"Lynn," I said. "I just wanted to tell you I'm sorry. For everything. Now I'm ready to make the changes I was too blind to make before. I know I'm too late to do that for you now, but I just wanted to thank you for showing me what they were."

She didn't say anything. She smiled softly, her eyes welling with tears.

"It was good seeing you, Lynn. Really."

And with that, I walked out of the room.

As part of the agreement, we were not allowed to do business in the industry for a period of three years from the time of the settlement. While that seemed like an easy punishment to endure, I have to admit that I missed not going to work and getting involved in a business that I had come to love. Time heals all wounds, as they say, and the more time passed, the more I learned to be content to be out of the rat race and spend my days with friends and family. As a younger man, I was consumed by work, by getting ahead, of making an impact in business. Granted, I was blessed to be self-employed and hugely successful and was able to have a lot of fun along the way, but there was still some part of me that wanted to get back into the trenches and get my hands dirty.

Nonetheless, these days my personal life is what I'm most passionate about. The business world is one of huge risks, and I took more than my share throughout my professional career. I'll never forget that pivotal moment when Ross first brought to me the concept of starting a cell phone business, and how I had first balked, content with climbing my way up the corporate ladder in the fast food industry. Now I must confess that I am enjoying the safe life I now lead. My days are spent the way I want to spend them. I am able to play golf at least 100 times a year, and I'm always on the lookout for anyone who can get me a tee time at Augusta! Each year, I treat my brother Martin and two of our closest friends to a golf trip. The four of us have enjoyed the challenging, beautiful courses of Pebble Beach, Pinehurst, TPC Sawgrass, Harbor Town, and Whistling Straits, among many others.

Lynn and I did get back together finally. There were some rough patches initially but they have all since been worked out. We had a baby girl named Jessica, and I was able to achieve perhaps the greatest goal I had set for myself – having a family. Together we enjoy travel and get away for a few days each month to spend quality time together. My daughter commands a great deal of attention. Watching her grow has been a blessing. Lynn and I have seen our little baby develop into an intelligent, precocious little girl who loves to do back handsprings and cheerlead. She also maintains a straight-A average in school, thanks to her mother's genes more than mine.

Ross has a new son who has grounded him and dulled the sharpness of his ambition. Still, he is not ready for full-time retirement. There will always be a part of him that wants more, whether that is to rise to the top of where he's at or start a whole new company and build it up to a powerhouse like he did with our two companies. He still works the phones like a madman, scouting the market for the next big thing. I often tell him he should send a resume to Donald Trump. He and the Donald could rule the world if they joined forces. He just smiles and shakes his head. He wants the world for himself and his child. And even though he talks a good game, I know he's at a place in his life where his son has given him a more precious set of priorities. I have little doubt that my nephew has a world of greatness ahead of him; the apple didn't fall too far from the tree in that family.

I still am close with those friends of mine that proved to be my real friends, who stuck it out with my brother and me during the good times and the bad. Every week Charles, Martin, Dorsey, Bart and I will get together for lunch, and it's like we are young men again; the jokes are fervent and the ribbing is endless. We play golf on a regular basis. We talk about everything from the "salad years" to what's going on with the new company. I have known Charles Sealey since my early days in Dallas, and he remains a close confidant, as well as my financial advisor. We speak daily and live in the same neighborhood.

When someone asks me how I got here – how my life reached this point after taking such turns and surviving the peaks and valleys as it did – I just smile at them and tell them that golf played a big part. They usually give me strange looks or laugh in a considerate but uncomprehending way. And really, the answer is as simple as a blade of finely trimmed grass.

Chasing the Green. It's what life is all about. It's the thing that pushes you to go beyond yourself, to strive for that one goal that perpetually seems out of reach and catapults you to reach out just enough to grab it.

So in the end, I ended up where I wanted to be in the first place. Because that's what *Chasing the Green* is all about. Finding what you love and pursuing it with all of your heart.

And that's all she wrote.

LaVergne, TN USA
09 March 2011
219432LV00002B/204/P